Forever After

Forever After

A Preplanned Passing is a Precious Gift

Paul James and Judith Hayes

Writer's Showcase
New York Lincoln Shanghai

Forever After
A Preplanned Passing is a Precious Gift

Writer's Showcase
an imprint of iUniverse, Inc.

For information address:
iUniverse
2021 Pine Lake Road, Suite 100
Lincoln, NE 68512
www.iuniverse.com

The information contained herein is for information purposes only, and should not be construed as financial or legal advice. Each state, county, and region has its own laws, rules, and regulations, and your individual state and local agencies should be consulted before making any decisions. Furthermore, the authors are neither financial nor legal experts, nor do they portray themselves as such. Consult with a certified financial planner or other financial advisor, as well as an attorney or other legal expert before acting on any information contained herein.

ISBN: 0-595-24981-7

Printed in the United States of America

For our mothers, Marian James and Edna Nickles, with love and affection. May you rest in peace.

It is better to spend your time at funerals than festivals. For you are going to die, and you should think about it while there is still time.

Ecclesiastes 7:2

A wise person thinks much about death, while the fool thinks only about having a good time now.

Ecclesiastes 7:4

CONTENTS

INTRODUCTION: If You Think You Don't Need to Plan,
Think Again! 1

PART 1: Making the Arrangements 7

ADVANCE HEALTH CARE DIRECTIVES 9
  What is a Living Will? 10
  What is a Health Care Surrogate Designation? 11
  Which is better? 11
  Do-Not-Resuscitate (DNR) Orders 12
  How Do I Make an Advance Directive? 13
  I Have an Advance Directive…Now What? 14

WILLS 21
  Why Do I Need a Will? 21
  How Do I Draft a Will? 23

FUNERAL PLANNING 25
  If I'm Not Dying, Why Should I Plan My Funeral? 25
  Pros and Cons of Preplanning 26
  Sales Techniques 27
  Steps to Preplanning 29
  Step One: Learn What Funeral Services are Available 29
  Step Two: Make the Arrangements 36
    More Questions to Ask 41

Flowers 43
Video 44
Judy on Women's Clothing 44
Paul on Men's Clothing 45
Step Three: Paying for Your Funeral 46

GENERATIONS TO COME 50

PART 2: Your Funeral Plans: Forms 53

General Instructions 55

Cover Letter 56

Living Will 57

Designation of Health Care Surrogate 60

Do Not Resuscitate Order 62

Notification List Instructions 64

Notification List 65

Funeral Wishes 69

Prepaid Burial Items List 72

Prepaid Cremation Items List 74

Documentation List 76

Business Card Holder 78

List of Financial Accounts 79

Special Gifts 81

Special Notes and Memories 82

PART 3: Survivors' Guide to Dealing with Death 87

YOUR LOVED ONE HAS DIED…NOW WHAT? 89

DEALING WITH GRIEF 91

DEALING WITH PROBATE 100

DEALING WITH MEDICAL BILLS & INSURANCE CLAIMS 103

DEALING WITH SURVIVOR BENEFITS 106
Social Security Administration Benefits 106
Who is Eligible? 106
Special One-Time Death Benefit 107
Veterans Administration (VA) Benefits 108
Who is Eligible? 108
How Much Can I Receive? 109
How Do I Apply? 109

APPENDICES 111

APPENDIX A: GLOSSARY 113

APPENDIX B: USEFUL WEBSITES 126

APPENDIX C: STATE LICENSING BOARDS 133

ENDNOTES 143

PREFACE

This book is for you if you want to plan your funeral so your loved ones aren't forced to make difficult decisions during possibly the worst time in their lives. We try in this book to lighten the load, to take a subject we all avoid thinking about—even though the death rate remains 100%—and make it bearable, even humorous sometimes. We hope our approach will help you complete your plans for the inevitable.

Our original vision for this book—one which we pray will come to fruition—is a design that will allow our readers to tailor it to their needs. With removable pages, fill-in-the-blank forms, journal pages, pockets, and a business card holder, our readers will be able to rearrange the pages in the order they prefer, write down memories or notes to cherished loved ones, and discard those (such as our stories) they deem irrelevant, the ultimate goal being to record in one place everything desired and necessary for their funerals. We ask that you pray for our success in this endeavor.

Until then, we recommend that you use this book to create your own planner, using this book, a three-ring notebook, or whatever works for you. Use the worksheets enclosed. Include in your planner copies of completed worksheets; copies of your will, living will, funeral contract, and other important documentation; and, business cards for your funeral director, attorney, financial consultant, and banker. This is important, not only to ensure your wishes will be met, but because it spares your loved ones of a lot of responsibility during their grief, and prevents them from having to make difficult decisions when they are most vulnerable. Though you may not realize it right now, your loved ones will consider your thoughtfulness and effort in this matter as your most precious gift.

Paul James and Judith Hayes,
South Florida
September, 2002

ACKNOWLEDGMENTS

We would like to thank our spouses, Joyce James and Shelby Hayes, for their continued support and encouragement throughout this project. We would like to thank God, for without His gifts and blessings and without His having brought us together, this book would have never been conceived. And, last but not least, Paul would like to thank his father, Donald James, for being his editor, cheerleader, and number-one fan during every one of the many unpublished years.

INTRODUCTION:
IF YOU THINK YOU DON'T NEED TO PLAN, THINK AGAIN!

Funerals cost big bucks. When you factor in grieving and all of the emotions that accompany it, funerals can cost even bigger bucks. According to the Federal Trade Commission (FTC),

> Funerals rank among the most expensive purchases many consumers will ever make. A traditional funeral, including a casket and vault, costs about $6,000, although "extras" like flowers, obituary notices, acknowledgment cards or limousines can add thousands of dollars to the bottom line. Many funerals run well over $10,000.[1]

That's one reason why planning is so important. Planning allows *you* to choose how much money you want to spend for your funeral. It also prevents your family from making unwise decisions in their time of grief.

Some bereaved feel money is no object, that the amount of money spent on a funeral is a reflection of how much they loved and honored the deceased. Funeral directors know this. While most funeral directors are kind and compassionate, funeral homes are businesses. They exist to make a profit. By having planned for your funeral, you've saved your loved ones from high pressure sales tactics, and from guilty feelings that may arise when they feel they haven't spent enough. Planning spares your loved ones additional grief, because all of the arrangements made were *your* decision.

I (Judy) have buried both of my parents. Both, fortunately, had pre-arranged funerals. My father died twelve years before my mother. He died on Sunday, July 3rd—a holiday weekend—which put everything on hold.

Mama insisted we take her to the funeral home on Monday to make sure the casket was exactly what Daddy had wanted. I refused to go inside. It was my first real experience with death and, after all, I was Daddy's little girl: I was a complete wreck.

The viewing was on Tuesday, July 6th, three days after Daddy had died. Though I was struggling to recover from the shock of seeing my beloved father in a coffin, I was "making nice" with relatives and friends when I saw a man I didn't recognize stopping here and there to chat with the guests. Lo and behold, he was a funeral home sales representative and he was trying to sell grave plots! Now, anger is one of the normal stages of the grieving process, but what I felt was pure rage. I immediately had the sales representative removed.

Mama had a prolonged illness, so, for her, there was more time to plan. Three to four months before she died, I called the same funeral home that had buried my father and told the director, point-blank, that I would not be in the day after Mama died because I knew about their gimmick, their gimmick being that even though Mama had prearranged her funeral, they would try to get me to upgrade in order to make extra profit.

Again, funeral homes are businesses. I don't blame them for wanting to make a profit. I just made it evident to the funeral director that she would not use my grief to leverage more profit from the deal. Furthermore, I impressed upon her that no one had better try selling anything at Mama's visitation. When everything was finally in place, my expectations were clear and I had not been pressured into any upgrades.

Mama died on December 31st, on a holiday weekend, like Daddy. Again, because of the holiday, we had to wait. But, because we had planned ahead, all was well. Or, so we thought.

During the visitation on Tuesday, the funeral director pulled me aside to tell me I owed her almost two hundred dollars for the announcements and death certificates. Because I wanted the opportunity to check the funeral contract, I told her I didn't have my checkbook with me. Though I don't condone lying, I had dealt with this funeral home before. And, as I had suspected, those fees had been prepaid.

*   *   *

Judy's parents preplanned their funerals, so her story illustrates how pre-planning your funeral will save your loved ones added expense and grief. Because my (Paul's) mother wasn't so thorough, my story shows in a different light how your wishes, if not clearly delineated, can consume your survivors as much as their loss. We conceived this planner for you because we realized how, for us, it would have been a Godsend.

In hindsight, I believe my mom knew she was dying, but "spared" my brothers and me the news. I believe this because, during the last few months of her life, she single-mindedly put her affairs in order. She rewrote her will, and had my brother Mark help her consolidate her bank and investment accounts. Prior to her death, it was all she would talk about.

After divorcing my father, Mom married a Frenchman I'll call Pierre. Before moving back to the United States, she lived with Pierre in Paris. Since they maintained bank accounts in both France and the United States, they made a verbal agreement between themselves stating that, in the event of their deaths, my brothers and I—and our children—would receive all funds in the U.S. accounts, while Pierre's children and grand-children would get all money in the France-based accounts. Mom had mentioned this verbal agreement to us many times and Pierre's children were aware of it, too.

During her marriage to Pierre, though, Mom had been completely frustrated by his children, often venting that *her* boys had maintained jobs from the time they were age 13, yet not one of his kids, now in their mid-40s, had ever held a job. Because of their intentional unemployment and expectation that Pierre and she should support them, Mom considered them to be lazy, irresponsible money-grubbers.

By French law, at least at that time, children had the rightful claim to their parents' assets, and could claim those assets even before their parents died. Pierre's children did just that. Although it was legal, Pierre and Mom never considered it moral; needless to say, they were furious. Vehement, Pierre assured his adult children that, because they had demanded their stakes early, they would not get a cent after he died.

So, just days before Pierre passed, his son flew in from France. His purpose was not to visit his father on his deathbed, but rather to persuade a neighbor to covertly convince Pierre to sign a form making him the sole beneficiary. The neighbor refused, then showed the form to Pierre. Fortunately. Signing that form would have rendered Mom homeless.

Mom grieved for Pierre for six months before passing on herself. Between Pierre's death and her own, Pierre's children aggressively attempted to persuade Mom to sign the France-based accounts over to them, referring inaccurately to the verbal agreement which specified how the assets would be distributed if *both* Pierre and Mom had died. As it stood, Mom was Pierre's widow and that money was rightfully hers.

Understandably, Mom was bitter. She felt Pierre's children had been bilking them for years, and most recently had tried to take her money and her home. She often said to me, "I'm not going to be here much longer," and wanted to ensure that they would not get "one dime of my children's money." She was so obsessed by this that, when her body was discovered, she was surrounded by a halo of legal papers. She literally had been planning for her passing right up to the second she died. However, because the plans she had completed were murky, settling her estate consumed us nearly as much as our grief.

First, amongst all the paperwork sat a paper shredder, which she had used. Pierre and Mom both had been heavy smokers and alcoholics; and, ultimately, their vices killed them both. Strangely, though Mom had kept intricate records (which she did not shred) on Pierre's declining health, not one datum of information about her own health remained. What else of importance had she mysteriously shredded?

Second, half of her paperwork had been written in French. None of us knew how to read French. Using French dictionaries Mom had owned, my brother Mark deciphered some of it, word by word, as he searched for a college student majoring in French to translate it for us. His crude translations identified some of those documents as life insurance policies. Were those policies still active? Were we entitled to any settlements?

Third, we found a list of numbers for bank accounts in the United States and France. Mark had helped Mom consolidate accounts, but he was not familiar with many of these. Which were still open and which were closed? Each had to be investigated. To gain access to the accounts in France, we figured we might need an attorney practicing in France. But what if those accounts had already been closed? If Mom had consolidated accounts to prevent Pierre's children from "getting a dime," why would there still *be* accounts open in France? Retaining a French attorney might glean or cost a fortune. Was the gamble worth it?

Fourth, there was a direct contradiction between Mom's stated desire that Pierre's kids not get a dime and the verbal agreement she often mentioned. The agreement was not annotated anywhere in their wills, but, then again, it was *verbal.* Did Pierre and Mom terminate that verbal agreement when Pierre's children claimed their inheritance antemortem? If so, why did Mom continue to mention it so often, right up to her death, years after that incident occurred? If not, did Mom then terminate the agreement when they tried to ruin her financially after Pierre's death? If she did, why, then, the existence of bank accounts in France, assuming they still existed? Why hadn't she transferred those funds to America? If those accounts were still open because she had died before she could close them, were Pierre's adult children entitled to those funds or were we?

Fifth, their wishes regarding Pierre's grandchildren were obscure. Their wills mentioned Mom's grandchildren, but were silent about Pierre's. True, Mom and Pierre were angry at his adult children, but did they really intend to punish Pierre's *grandchildren* for behavior they had nothing to do with?

As you can see, in settling Mom's estate many questions plagued us, and each question begged three more. I pray that my story clarifies this point: When both parents die, disputes between extended families may drain both sides, emotionally and financially, but imagine how devastating disputes over money can be *within* a family. I thank God for my brothers, Greg and Mark! Greed could have easily bitten any one of us, but, fortunately, we acted as a family should. My story should make it evident to you why planning your passing is the most precious gift you will ever give to your loved ones. Once you have done so, your family is safe.

PART 1:

Making the Arrangements

ADVANCE HEALTH CARE DIRECTIVES

While it is critical to make arrangements for after your death, it is equally important to plan for what happens to you *before* you die, should you become incapacitated and unable to tell your physician how you want to be treated. You do this with an advance directive.

An *advance directive* is an oral or written statement, witnessed in advance of serious illness or injury, that specifies what kind of treatment you want under serious medical conditions, or names someone to make those decisions for you. A good advance directive describes the kind of treatment you would want for different degrees of illness.[2]

If you don't have an advance directive naming a surrogate or proxy, health care decisions may be made for you by someone else, contrary to your wishes. Usually, the court will designate a default surrogate, typically in order of kinship. For example, if you are a resident of Florida and do not have an advance directive naming a surrogate, medical decisions will be made for you by a court-appointed guardian, your spouse, your adult child, your parent, your adult sibling, an adult relative, or a close friend—in that order.[3] Take a moment to look at that again. Did you notice that in Florida a court-appointed guardian, whomever that might be, has precedence over your *spouse?* Though Florida allows it, be aware that few states authorize a close friend to make decisions for you, and then only when family members are unavailable.

Have we mentioned our belief that this planner, once completed, will be the most precious gift you'll ever give your family, that having all of the arrangements for your funeral in place will spare your family from having to make gut-wrenching decisions after you die? Imagine how much grief you'll spare them when you have an advance directive! Doctors and health care facilities routinely rely on family involvement in decision making. What if your loved ones don't know what you would want in any given situation? What if they disagree about the best course of action? Can you imagine how that would rip your family apart? Can you imagine their needless agony over being forced to make life or death decisions without clear guidance from you? Protect them from all of that! Make sure you have advance directives.

Laws about advance directives vary from state to state, so be aware of the guidelines and technical requirements in your state.

In Florida, the two most common advance directives are:

- the Living Will, and

- the Health Care Surrogate Designation.[4]

Health Care Surrogate Designations may also be known in other states as Health Care Powers of Attorney, Health Care Proxies, and Durable Powers of Attorney for Health Care.

What is a Living Will?

A *living will* specifies the kind of medical care you want or do not want if you are unable to make your own decisions. It is called a "living" will because it takes effect while you are still living. A living will *only takes effect when you are terminally ill,* which generally means you have less than six months to live.[5]

Most state statutes provide suggested forms for living wills, but in most states, the forms are optional. In about 18 states, the forms must be substantially followed, or certain information disclosure language must be included.[6] Changes and additions to standard language are permissible, however, because a living will should be personalized to reflect your values, priorities and wishes. Therefore, unless it truly reflects your specific wishes, don't just sign an "official" form unchanged. If changing the wording creates any doubt about the validity of the form, then seek legal consultation.

As an example, the living will form included in the Florida statutes is provided in Figure 1. You may wish to consult with your physician or attorney to ensure you have completed your living will in a way that will ensure your wishes are understood.

What is a Health Care Surrogate Designation?

A Health Care Surrogate Designation (also known as Health Care Power of Attorney, Health Care Proxy, or Durable Power of Attorney for Health Care) is a form naming another person as your agent or proxy to make medical decisions for you, if you should become unable to make them yourself. It becomes active any time you are unconscious or are unable to make medical decisions. In a health care surrogate designation, you may also include instructions regarding medical treatment you want or wish to avoid.

Florida statutes provide a suggested form, an example of which is shown in Figure 2. Again, your state likely will have its own suggested form to which you may make changes or additions. Make sure that your completed health care surrogate designation is in compliance with your state laws.

Which is better?

A living will, by itself, is not the document most people need[7]. In a living will, you can describe the kinds of treatment you wish to receive or avoid in certain situations, but it does not allow you to select someone to make decisions for you. Also, a living will only becomes effective when you become terminally ill or permanently unconscious. Most standard living will forms are limited in what they cover and what they can accomplish.

Health care surrogate designations allow you to specify what treatments you wish to receive or avoid in certain situations, and allow you to specify a surrogate who knows your values intimately to act as your legal decision maker, spokesperson, and advocate. If there is no one close whom you trust to make medical decisions for you, a health care surrogate designation should not be used; in this circumstance, a living will is a safer bet, despite its limitations[8].

You may wish to have both a living will and a health care surrogate designation, or, depending on the state in which you live, you may combine them into a single document. In either case, make sure that the documents, whether separate or combined, describe treatment choices in a variety of situations, and name someone to make decisions for you should you be unable to make decisions for yourself.

Do-Not-Resuscitate (DNR) Orders

Some patients decide they won't benefit from cardiopulmonary resuscitation (CPR) if, for example, they have a terminal illness. Unless the hospital staff has been given other instructions, it will try to resuscitate all patients whose hearts or breathing have stopped. If you don't want CPR, you can communicate your wish in an advance directive or by discussing it with your doctor. In either case, your doctor will put a Do-Not-Resuscitate (DNR) order, or DNR, in your medical chart. See Figure 3 for an example of a DNR. Because the DNR form is yellow, it stands out among the white pages of a medical chart. DNRs are accepted by doctors and hospitals in all states[9].

*   *   *

When Mama was discharged from the hospital after open-heart surgery, she and I (Judy) were visiting a friend when the subject of advance health care directives came up in conversation. Mama was adamant about never going on life support, so after discussing the pros and cons of living wills and health care surrogates, she insisted we complete these forms as soon as possible. Once Mama signed a health care surrogate designation and a living will, we were "cool," or so we thought.

Six months later, after being admitted to the hospital, Mama developed pneumonia. Overnight, her lungs filled with fluid and by morning, when the nurse was making her rounds, she was nearly gone. Fortunately, the staff had been able to stabilize Mama without putting her on a ventilator. Mama's medical chart noted that she had a living will, but the hospital did not have a copy. The nurse called me and advised me to bring one to the hospital immediately. Imagine our surprise when we discovered the living will's terminally ill clause, which stated it only became effective if Mama was diagnosed with cancer or some other terminal illness. She'd only had pneumonia…and I'd had false security.

Mama was as fearful of being on life support as I was of having to "pull the plug." So, together we discovered and signed a DNR. As Mama's illness progressed, she was in and out of hospitals, nursing homes and assisted living facilities. We made sure that every facility had a copy of her DNR. I even kept one in my purse when she stayed at my house, just in case I ever had to call 911. I had no intention of ever having to make a decision to pull the plug.

It has been my experience that most documents pertaining to health care are missing something. It is not always clear what that "something" is. With that in mind, read the fine print carefully. Know what it means. If you don't understand something, consult an attorney. In any case, make your wishes known. It may be your last chance.

How Do I Make an Advance Directive?

First, obtain an official form provided in your state statutes, if available, and one or two advance directive forms from other sources. This will help you see how different forms handle different topics. Realize that, because people are different, there is no perfect form for everyone.

Second, collect information on your current medical condition and its implications for future medical problems. Clarify your own values and wishes, then discuss them with your close family, your physician, and your intended surrogate. Find out whether they are willing to support you the way you want.

Third, complete the forms you choose, making sure to modify the language to specifically suit your needs. Follow the witnessing instructions for your state exactly.[10]

I Have an Advance Directive...Now What?

- Keep copies of your advance directives in your planner, so that they can be easily found.

- If you have a designated health care surrogate or proxy, give him or her the original or a copy.

- Give a copy to your physician for your medical file.

- Keep a card or note in your purse or wallet, stating that you have an advance directive, and where it is located.

- If you make changes, make sure those concerned have the latest copy.[11]

Living Will[12]

Declaration made this ___day of _____, 20__, I, _____, willfully and voluntarily make known my desire that my dying not be artificially prolonged under the circumstances set forth below, and I do hereby declare that, if at any time I am mentally or physically incapacitated

___*(initial)* and I have a terminal condition

or ___*(initial)* and I have an end-state condition

or ___*(initial)* and I am in a persistent vegetative state

and if my attending or treating physician and other consulting physician have determined that there is no reasonable medical probability of my recovery from such condition, I direct that life-prolonging procedures be withheld or withdrawn with the application of such procedures would serve only to prolong artificially the process of dying, and that I be permitted to die naturally with only the administration of medication or the performance of any medical procedure deemed necessarily to provide me with comfort care or to alleviate pain.

It is my intention that this declaration be honored by my family and physician as the final expression of my legal right to refuse medical or surgical treatment and to accept the consequences for such refusal.

In the event I have been determined to be unable to provide express and informed consent regarding the withholding, withdrawal, or continuation of life-prolonging procedures, I wish to designate, as my surrogate to carry out the provisions of this declaration:

Name:_____

Address:_____

_____Zip Code:_____

Phone:_____

I understand the full import of this declaration, and I am emotionally and mentally competent to make this declaration.

Additional instructions (optional):

_____

_____

_____

(Signed)

_____   _____

(Witness)   *(Witness)*

_____   _____

(Address)   *(Address)*

_____   _____

(Phone)   *(Phone)*

(At least one witness must be neither a spouse nor a blood relative of the signatory.)

Figure 1

Designation of Health Care Surrogate[13]

Name:_____

     (Last Name)   *(First Name)*   *(Middle Initial)*

In the event that I have been determined to be incapacitated to provide informed consent for medical treatment and surgical and diagnostic procedures, I wish to designate as my surrogate for health care decisions:

Name: _____

Address:_____Zip Code: _____

Phone: _____

If my surrogate is unwilling or unable to perform his or her duties, I wish to designate as my alternate surrogate:

Name: _____

Address:_____Zip Code: _____

Phone: _____

I fully understand that this designation will permit my designee to make health care decisions and to provide, withhold, or withdraw consent on my behalf; to apply for public benefits to defray cost of health care; and to authorize my admission to or transfer from a health care facility.

Additional instructions (optional):

_____

_____

_____

_____

I further affirm that this designation is not being made a condition of treatment or admission to a health care facility. I will notify and send a copy of this document to the following persons other than my surrogate, so they may know who my surrogate is.

Name:_____

Name:_____

Signed:_____Date:_____

Witnesses: 1._____

2._____

(At least one witness must be neither a spouse nor a blood relative of the signatory.)

Figure 2

FLORIDA
DO NOT RESUSCITATE ORDER

(Please use ink)

Patient's Full Legal Name_____   _____
                              (Print or Type Name)   (Date)

PATIENT'S STATEMENT

Based upon informed consent, I, the undersigned, hereby direct that CPR be withheld or withdrawn. **(If not signed by patient, check applicable box):**

☐ Surrogate   ☐ Proxy (both as defined in Chapter 765, F. S.)

☐ Court appointed guardian   ☐ Durable power of attorney (pursuant to Chapter 709, F. S.)

_____

(Applicable Signature)   (Print or Type Name)

PHYSICIAN'S STATEMENT

I, the undersigned, a physician licensed pursuant to Chapter 458 or 459, F. S., am the physician of the patient named above. I hereby direct the withholding or withdrawing of cardiopulmonary resuscitation (artificial ventilation, cardiac compression, endotracheal intubation, and defibrillation) from the patient in the event of the patient's cardiac or respiratory arrest.

_____

(Signature of Physician)　　　　　(Date)　　　　Telephone Number (Emergency)

_____

(Print or Type Name)　　　　　　　　(Physician's Medical License Number)

Pursuant to s.401.45, F. S., a copy or original of this DNRO may be honored by hospital emergency services, nursing homes, assisted living facilities, home health agencies, hospices, adult family-care, and emergency medical services.

Figure 3

WILLS

Since a will is not read until after a funeral, you do not want to rely on your will to ensure your funeral plans are carried out. You should use your planner for that. And, since your planner is designed to ensure *all* of your wishes are carried out after you die, you should keep a copy of your will in it.

Why Do I Need a Will?[14]

It is critical that you have a will. If you don't:

- *State law will determine what happens to your property.* This process is called *intestate succession.*[15] If you fail to choose an executor to ensure your property is distributed according to your wishes, the court will appoint an administrator, for a fee. The administrator will distribute your money and belongings to your spouse and children, or if you have neither, to other relatives, according to state law. If the administrator can't find relatives to inherit your property, your property will go to the state.

- *Your spouse may not get enough money to make ends meet,* if you fail to specifically ensure he or she gets enough with which to live comfortably.

- *Your assets may be divided equally among your heirs, if there is no surviving spouse.* You may not want this to happen if, for example, one adult child is well off while another child needs financial assistance. If you haven't drafted a will, you won't be able to help.

- *Your grandchildren may not get a penny.* If you have no will, most state courts will grant an estate's assets first to the surviving spouse, then the children, often leaving out the generation after. If you have no will, you can't allocate assets to your grandchildren through a trust, and can't name a guardian to manage their financial affairs until they're mature enough to do so on their own.

- *Your stepchildren may not get a cent.* Because most states define heirs as "blood" relatives, stepchildren may not be recognized as heirs, unless a stepchild has been legally adopted. Having a will can ensure your stepchildren are not left out.

- *You may not get the guardian you want for your minor children.* If you don't have a will, the court will determine who will care for your children if the other parent is unavailable or unfit. If both parents have passed, grandparents are the natural guardians of minor children. Which set of grandparents? The court will decide. If you shudder at the thought of your children being raised by your in-laws, you certainly have sufficient motivation for drafting a will.

- *You can't minimize estate taxes your children or other heirs might have to pay.* You and your spouse can shelter as much as $1.3 million of assets from federal estate taxes by setting up trusts within your wills.[16] To do so, you will need the help of a lawyer.

- *You can't give specific things to favorite people.* With a will, and an adjoining letter of intent, you can specify who gets what. A *letter of intent* is a list of items with corresponding beneficiaries. In some states, letters of intent can be changed from time to time without having to redraft the will. It's a good way to avoid family fights.

- *You can't give to a church or charity.* Because state laws don't consider religious or charitable organizations as heirs, your will is the only way to ensure your church or favorite charity gets a donation.

- *A family member receiving Medicaid benefits may lose them.* Medicaid has strict income qualifications. If money is paid from your estate to a parent or family member receiving Medicaid benefits while in a nursing facility, the additional income may disqualify your loved one from continuing to receive benefits.

How Do I Draft a Will?

Drafting a will is a relatively simple task. Whether or not you need an attorney to draft one is your decision. Many people use good self-help books or software packages to draft simple wills, but if your situation is more complex, it may be wise to seek legal counsel. There are just a few technical requirements for a will to be legal:

- It must be typewritten or computer generated. However, in about 25 states "holographic," or handwritten, wills are legal.[17] To be valid, holographic wills must be written, dated and signed in the handwriting of the person making the will.

- It must explicitly state that it is your will.

- It must be signed and dated by you.

- It must be signed by at least two witnesses whom have watched you sign it. Some states require three witnesses.[18]

Your will is not required to be notarized or filed with the court. However, in some situations and in some states, you may do so. Just keep your original will in a safe, accessible place, and keep a copy in your planner. Make sure the person handling your affairs after you die knows where they are.

DID YOU KNOW?

Though some funeral homes may include the word "society" in their names, they are not nonprofit organizations.[19] Rather, they may be for-profit companies.

FUNERAL PLANNING

If I'm Not Dying, Why Should I Plan My Funeral?

To answer that question, we hate to say it, but you *are* dying—every single day. The death rate currently stands at 100% in every nation on earth, even the good old United States of America. Therefore, it is a great idea to plan your funeral while you are still healthy.

Before diving in, though, you need to be aware of some terminology used by the funeral industry. Though the terms used sound similar, they can have significantly different meanings, especially when it comes to money. *Preplanning* is just what it sounds like: planning ahead for your death. When preplanning, you decide, for example, whether you want to be buried or cremated, or whether you want your grave marker to be made of marble or granite. Preplanning, however, does not consider how your plans will be paid for. *Prearranging*, on the other hand, does. Prearranging *seems* like it would mean the same thing as preplanning, but it actually comprises preplanning and *prefunding*, which entails different methods of investing and paying for it all. The key, here, is to research fully. Do not sign any contracts until you have fully read and completely understand them.

Pros and Cons of Preplanning

There are absolutely no cons to *preplanning*, as defined above. Preplanning is one of the kindest things you can do for yourself and your family. Benefits of preplanning include the following:

- It gives you time to research funeral providers and prices and, thus, make informed decisions.

- It permits you to personalize your service, making it as simple or traditional as you want.

- By eliminating second-guessing by your survivors, it ensures your wishes will be met.

- It prevents your loved ones from overspending resulting from grief, guilt and other strong emotions.

- It spares your loved ones a tremendous emotional burden on possibly the worst day of their lives.[20]

Though there are only pros to preplanning, paying for your funeral ahead of time should be considered very carefully. In fact, *Consumer Reports Online* ("Final Arrangements," May 2001)[21] strongly advises consumers to stay away from these plans altogether. Its study revealed that prepaying for funerals benefits funeral homes, not consumers. The pitch is simple: Plan ahead to save your family the stress of making arrangements at the worst time, and lock in your price now to avoid much higher costs later. According to *Consumer Reports Online*, not only will you *not* save money, it is highly likely that you will overpay because you will be charged higher prices for the value you will receive.

You may decide you want to prepay anyway. That way, your funeral is planned and paid for, and you will have peace-of-mind knowing that your family is spared the burden of making those decisions while they're grieving. Certainly, that is an honorable and loving motive for paying ahead of time. Just be aware that saving money is not a sound reason for paying ahead. Again, do your research. Ask lots of questions. Don't sign anything until you fully understand it. And, beware of sales pitches.

Sales Techniques

Funeral homes are businesses, plain and simple. No one can blame them for wanting to make a profit. In fact, like any other business, they *need* to make a profit to survive. Of course, there are some less-than-ethical funeral providers and you need to be alert to the possibility that you just might be dealing with one of them. However, you also need to be aware that ethical funeral providers don't deserve a sleazy image just for trying to make a living. Though high-pressure salespeople give *all* salespeople a bad name, funeral sales professionals undeservedly get a doubly bad name because, due to the nature of their business, they sell to people who are in pain. Remember, most want to help you. But in order to get your business, they have to use sales techniques, just like the local realtor who mails you post cards every day and plants American flags in your front yard every Fourth of July (no one trashes *them*!). Nevertheless, it is your job to be an informed consumer and to be aware of what funeral providers are doing when they offer you free stuff.

One technique that funeral providers use is to make a charitable contribution in the deceased's name, or to plant a tree in his or her memory. This gives a salesperson a legitimate excuse to call you after the funeral, so that he or she can insist on delivering the certificate in person. Once you agree to this, it gives the sales rep an opportunity to sit down with you in your home, get feedback about the funeral, and attempt to sell you on a preneed contract.

A second technique is to offer planning guides. Planning guides are a good thing! That's what this book is all about. How preneed sellers use planning guides, however, is to present them in a group setting and tell everyone that the books are all out of stock right now (in which case, you should immediately recommend that everyone in the group buy a copy of this one and advise the presenter that they never run out of copies of *Forever After* at Barnes and Noble), but he or she would be glad to personally deliver a copy to your home. Personal delivery, of course, get the salesperson in the door.

A third technique is called cloverleafing. Cloverleafing is used by all successful salespeople in every profession. When I (Paul) was a sales rep, we called it "one stop, three drops." What that meant was, once I closed a sale, I would drop off business cards to the neighbors on each side of my new customer. Think about it. Who is more likely to buy than someone who sees how happy their neighbor is with their new purchase, because whatever product or service they just bought makes their life easier and less stressful? Preneed salespeople are no different if they want to be successful, because people are more receptive to hearing about funerals and grave sites when there has been a death in the neighborhood.

A fourth technique is the use of thank-you notes. The salesperson provides you with thank-you notes, and volunteers to pick them up, stamp them, and mail them out for you. Before mailing out the notes, however, he or she copies the names and addresses, thereby generating a list of prospects. Again, the premise is that those stung by the death of a relative or friend are more likely to receptive to a preneed sales presentation.

A fifth technique is to offer free cemetery plots. The goal, here, is to sell additional services and merchandise, such as a plot for your spouse, for example.

A sixth technique is to request a list of ten best friends, so that your friends can be informed in the event of your death. Of course, this technique is used to generate a list of prospects, and you can tell them you have already taken care of that by using this book (shameless, we know).

Of course, there are many other sales techniques out there, and some are not legitimate at all. Keep your eyes and ears open. Ask a lot of questions. Don't sign anything until you understand *exactly* what you are signing.

Steps to Preplanning

Preplanning your funeral is a three-step process.[22] First, you must learn about funeral services so you can decide what type of funeral you want and how much you can afford. Second, you must make the arrangements by way of a preneed funeral contract, including all the goods and services that will be required. And, third, you must fund the cost of your funeral either through a regulated trust, life insurance, personal savings, certificate of deposit account designated for funeral expenses, or some other method. *It is possible to select funeral goods and services without prefunding them.* It is also possible to prefund a funeral without choosing specific goods and services.[23] Be aware, though, that should you choose either of these options, the price of your funeral usually will not be guaranteed.

Step One: Learn What Funeral Services are Available

Funerals commemorate lives that have been lived, and offer family and friends opportunities to pay tribute to their love ones. The gathering of family and friends helps the grieving face the reality of death, and offers them emotional support in taking the first steps toward resolving their grief. The funeral is a ceremony of proven worth for those who will mourn you. The type of service conducted is typically selected by the family in the absence of preplanning, but, in your case, it will be selected by *you*.

My (Judy's) father had a *traditional funeral*, but not by choice. When Daddy passed, Mama and he had lived in Florida for only a short period of time, and had not yet found a church home with which they felt comfortable. So, with his passing, it was my responsibility to find a pastor that would perform the ceremony.

Being desperate, but not wanting to deal with it because I was grieving, I took the easy way out and called the pastor of my church. The pastor came to my house where the family had gathered to discuss what he would say at the funeral. We provided him with some general statistics and personal facts, around which he build his sermon. The pastor had never met my father.

In church, the pastor offered a brief description of Daddy's life, a reading of the Scriptures, and a prayer. At the grave site, he quoted some more Bible verses and said another prayer. Daddy's funeral was very sad. And, very short. It is expected that the family pay clergy for their services. The amount is usually left up to the discretion of the family. After Daddy's funeral, I had my husband slip my pastor a check.

A *celebration of life funeral* is an alternative. It's just what it sounds like: celebrating the life of a loved one rather than grieving his or her passing. I think most of our loved ones who have passed would rather we do that.

When Mama passed, we had a celebration of life funeral, but we really didn't plan it that way. It was truly special. Her grandchildren had things to say to her, and read poems they had written for her. The pastor (my nephew) had known Mama all of his life, so he had lots of funny stories to share about their time together. My favorite was, "You guys stop your crying. Don't use up all the Kleenex. They cost a lot of money!" This was a big laugh for the family, as Mama was especially frugal. As we celebrated her life, we paused to look forward to the celebration we will someday share with her and our Lord Jesus Christ. Because her funeral was upbeat, uplifting, even funny at times, Mama would have loved it.

I, too, want my funeral to be a joyous occasion. I will have left the ways of the world behind and passed on to Heaven, where angels sing and I won't have to answer the phone ever again! So, I want my family to honor me not with tears and sadness, but with laughter and joy. Because I brought my children up in the church, I want a pastor to preside over my funeral to comfort them. Because my children are strong-willed and argue a lot about nothing, I want his sermon to be about loving and caring for one another.

Finally, instead of a funeral at all, you might opt for a *memorial service*. At a memorial service, the body is not in attendance. This service can be a celebration of life, a candlelight ceremony or a mix of traditional (with pastor conducting) and celebration of life.

Memorial services are popular if a prominent citizen has moved and died in another part of the country. The actual funeral and burial can be held in the town in which the person passed, while the memorial service is held in the town in which he or she lived most of his or her life.

My husband, Shelby, had a very close and extremely wealthy friend from up north, who had spent his winters in Florida. He had a lengthy illness and, because he passed away in Vermont, was unable to say goodbye to many of his Floridian friends. A couple of months after his death, a memorial service was held in Florida at a private club on the beach. His friends had an opportunity to say goodbye, drink a toast, share nice things about him, and have lunch. What a celebration! It made everyone remember how he had touched their lives and how much we would all dearly miss him.

Memorial services are usually held for someone who has been cremated, in that you can take the ashes and scatter them where the deceased has requested.

Cremation is an alternative to being buried, and is gaining popularity in the United States. Cremation is a process that reduces the body and its container to ashes and fragments by applying intense heat. Among people who died in 1999, 24% were cremated. The top states for cremation were Nevada (61.1%) and Alaska (58.5%), while those with the lowest rates were West Virginia (4.9%) and Mississippi (5.0%).[24] Cremation is expected to rise in popularity. According to *USA Today*, the rate will approach 40% by the year 2010, and will become the normal method of disposing bodies. For 2010, the Cremation Association of North America predicts 36.06%.[25]

One of the reasons cremation is becoming more popular is because some people are deciding that they don't want to spend thousands of dollars on elaborate funerals. It used to be that funerals were milestones in one's life worthy of great expense, much like weddings are now, but the trend is gradually turning toward cheaper alternatives. Cremation can be more economical than burial, because a simple container can be used in place of an expensive casket and there are no costs associated with the perpetual care of a grave site.

There are other advantages, as well. Cremated remains may be scattered in a place of significance to the deceased, for example, during a memorial service. Some people would rather have their body consumed quickly by fire rather than allowing it to decay in a grave. Some people cite environmental concerns, or don't want their grave to occupy badly needed land.

Yet for others, for religious reasons cremation remains taboo. While cremation is common in Hindu and Buddhism, it remains a subject of controversy to Christians.[26] Verses in the Old Testament show that the burning of bodies and objects in ancient Israel was mostly reserved for idols, criminals or enemies, yet the New Testament contains few references of this practice. Throughout the Scriptures, however, failure to be given a proper burial is considered to be a great tragedy and dishonor.

In the New Testament, 1 Corinthians 15 indicates that burial is proper for Christians. The Bible says that when Jesus Christ was resurrected, he became the first of a great harvest of those who will be raised to life again (1 Cor. 15: 20).

*   *   *

But someone may ask, "How will the dead be raised? What kind of bodies will they have?" What a foolish question! When you put a seed into the ground, it doesn't grow into a plant unless it dies first. And what you put in the ground is not the plant that will grow, but only a dry little seed of wheat or whatever it is you are planting. Then God gives it a new body—just the kind he wants it to have. (1 Cor. 15: 35-38)

*   *   *

Our earthly bodies, which die and decay, will be different when they are resurrected, for they will never die. Our bodies now disappoint us, but when they are raised, they will be full of glory. They are weak now, but when they are raised, they will be full of power. They are natural human bodies now, but when they are raised, they will be spiritual bodies. For just as there are natural bodies, so also there are spiritual bodies. (1 Cor. 15: 42-44)

*   *   *

Flesh and blood cannot inherit the Kingdom of God. These perishable bodies of ours are not able to live forever...Christians who have died will be raised with transformed bodies. And then we who are living will be transformed so that we will never die. For our perishable earthly bodies must be transformed into heavenly bodies that will never die. (1 Cor. 15: 50-54)

*   *   *

The Christian controversy over cremation remains. If you are a Christian, you should give great consideration to your decision on whether to be cremated or buried.

There is a specific nomenclature that describes cremation. *Cremains*, or cremated remains, are the ashes and bone fragments that remain after cremation is complete. The cremains are usually kept in an *urn*, rather than a casket, and rather than being buried in a plot, there are several options for internment of cremains.

A *columbarium* is an indoor or outdoor wall containing *niches*, which are recessed compartments designed to hold urns. Columbariums may be a whole building, a room, a single wall, or a series of halls in a mausoleum or chapel. Niches vary in size also, and may have glass, marble, bronze, or granite fronts.[27]

Many cemeteries or memorial parks have areas designated for the internment of cremains, called *urn gardens*. Urn gardens are for those who desire ground or above-ground internment, and some offer individual urn burial plots that will accommodate a marker.[28]

Some cemeteries have opened *scattering gardens*, where loved ones may scatter ashes. The names of those whose remains have been scattered in the garden are inscribed on a memorial plaque, wall or work of art.[29]

Keepsake urns and *keepsake jewelry* are available to hold a small portion of the cremains, when only a portion of the ashes will be scattered, or when family members opt to divide the cremains among themselves. Cremains can be permanently embedded in glass sculptures, or integrated into memorial tablets which may be placed in a church or memorial garden or in the ground.[30]

*   *   *

I (Paul) will never forget the day my brothers and I went to the crematorium to make final arrangements for my mother. Our "counselor," i.e., sales representative, while incredibly insensitive in a lot of ways, was invaluable in helping us make Mom's final arrangements. Dealing with death was an area in which we were completely inexperienced, and for which we were totally unprepared.

Our counselor advised us that, when they transported Mom to the crematorium from the morgue, she would be nude. "Would she have wanted to be cremated in a special dress?" the counselor asked. How would *we* know? For some reason—grief, shock, whatever—we never realized she would be *nude*! When we agreed that, yes, she would have wanted to be dressed in *something*, the counselor advised us to select a dress with a high neckline. Mom had been through an autopsy, she warned us. We wouldn't want to see *that*.

Though each of us would break down at least once during the consultation, our counselor plodded through her presentation like an automaton. I spent many years in sales and one of the first things I learned was that in order to be successful, a sales representative must learn to *listen*. Not only was she not listening, she was so intent on completing her paperwork (and closing the sale) that she was not even looking. Not only was she not empathetic, she wasn't even aware we were crying! Now, I realize that cremation is her industry, that after many years she may have become numb to the grief or found it necessary to disengage her emotions. Fine. But, I also know that if anyone needs to at least *appear* empathetic, it would be someone in her profession!

After much of the paperwork had been completed—and our counselor had been unsuccessful in selling us a $5,000 casket to torch—she decided to "up" the sales pressure. Certainly, an expensive urn had possibility. When we advised her that Mom wanted her ashes spread in Hawaii, that there was no need for an urn, she pushed even harder for a keepsake urn, one in which we could "keep just a part of" Mom around. Finally frustrated with her aggressive sales tactics and the morbidity of it all, I lost my temper.

To emphasize the absolute importance of thorough preplanning, at least, I must share with you how pitiful Mom's funeral was. Due to complete prearrangement, those who loved Judy's mother were able, at her funeral, to celebrate her life. My mom prearranged her funeral, too, so to speak, in that she prepaid for her cremation. But that was it. To this day, my memory of her funeral service crushes me. The "service" was far, far less than she deserved.

There were few there that day to say goodbye, just my brothers, my wife, myself, and a minister whom we paid to be there. In life, Mom was a beautiful woman. In a cardboard box, with no makeup and her hair undone, she looked like hell. I wanted nothing more than to touch her, to hug her, to tell her I loved and missed her, but we were advised not to touch her lest the autopsy incisions come undone.

No eulogies were given by her sons because, really, there was no one to give them to but ourselves. We shed a lot of tears and merely said goodbye. The minister, I'm sure, said something, but I can't remember him being there with us. Mom died before I became a Christian, but I think I may have prayed. In under ten minutes, it was done. We left the crematorium in silence.

The manner in which Mom lived the last years of her life and the absolute needlessness of her death made me realize there is so much more to life than merely existing. In the agonizing months following her death, I finally found peace in God.

Step Two: Make the Arrangements

One of your first decisions will be to select a funeral home or crematorium. Where you want your final resting place to be will play a major role in your choice. Make a list of questions you want answered, then take it with you. Don't select a funeral home or crematorium at your first interview, just to get this task over with quickly as possible. Give this decision a great deal of thought!

When we're looking to buy a new car or appliance, we like to look for the best deal. Have you ever thought about shopping around for your funeral? Strange, isn't it? Yet that is exactly what you need to do. Prices vary widely, so shopping around can save you thousands of dollars.

There is some controversy over the funeral industry. Funeral directors, whether fairly or not, have to overcome the image of swindlers squeezing the bereaved for every dollar they can.[31] As is true in every industry, there are some whose lack of ethics make it harder for the rest. If you inform yourself before ever setting foot in a funeral director's office, you won't easily be taken advantage of. Our aim here is to provide you with some basic information, but funeral requirements may vary from state to state. Do your homework.

Fortunately, there is a federal law to protect you, and make your job a little easier. It's called the Funeral Rule and it is enforced by the Federal Trade Commission (FTC).[32] The Funeral Rule requires funeral directors to give you itemized prices in person and over the phone, if you ask. If you ask about arrangements in person, funeral directors must give you a written price list that shows goods and services the funeral home offers. This is yours to keep. If you ask about a casket or outer burial container, the Funeral Rule requires the provider to show you descriptions of available selections and prices *before* showing you the caskets. Furthermore, while funeral providers offer various funeral packages, you have the right to purchase individual goods and services. In other words, you do not have to accept a package that includes items you do not want.

According to the Funeral Rule[33]:

- You have the right to choose the goods and services you want (with some exceptions);

- The funeral provider must state this right in writing on the general price list (see definition below);

- If state or local law requires you to purchase any particular item, it must be disclosed on the price list with reference to a specific law; and,

- A funeral provider that offers cremations must have alternative containers available.

It is important to realize that state and local laws vary. Check the laws in your state.

In several states, only a licensed funeral director can prearrange your funeral.[34] Check the credentials of the person selling the preneed funeral contract. If that person is not affiliated with a funeral home, ask to see a copy of the agreement between the seller and the funeral home you select. A copy of the agreement should be included with the contract.

A preneed contract should clearly state whether your funeral will be guaranteed or not guaranteed.[35] The existence or lack of a guarantee has to do with the *price* of the funeral. When your funeral is guaranteed, your loved ones will not be required to pay any more money for your funeral, regardless of the price of the funeral when you die. Be aware, though, that if you prepay your funeral expenses, you may actually pay much more than if you hadn't. In any case, make sure it is in writing.

The *professional* or *basic services fee*, as defined by the FTC, is allowable coverage for the basic services of the funeral director and staff, furnished by the funeral provider in arranging any funeral, such as conducting the arrangements conference, planning the funeral, obtaining necessary permits, and placing obituary notices. It is the only funeral provider fee permitted for services, facilities or unallocated overhead. It is nondeclinable, unless otherwise permitted by law. The professional or basic services fee is the funeral home's cost of doing business. It is *in addition* to the goods and services you select.[36]

The *general price list* contains the current cost of, and disclosures about, individual goods and services offered. The FTC requires funeral homes to provide you with a general price list.[37]

The FTC also requires funeral homes to provide you with an itemized *statement of goods and services*, which allows you to evaluate your decisions and make changes. This statement must clearly identify what goods and services are required, explain why they are required, provide cost information, and include required disclosures regarding legal requirements, embalming and cash advance items (goods and services obtained from a third party by the funeral home).[38]

The preneed funeral contract should contain a complete description and current price of the goods and services you are purchasing. It should include clear answers to the following questions:[39]

- What are the rights and obligations of all parties to the contract?

- What is the relationship between the entity providing the funding and the funeral home providing the goods and services?

- Who is the seller, the purchaser and the person for whom the contract is purchased?

- In detail, what goods and services are required?

- What specific type of funding plan is agreed to?

- To what extent are the prices of itemized goods and services guaranteed?

- If selected goods or services are not available at the time of need, will they be substituted—at no cost—with goods or services of equal or greater value?

- What are the geographical boundaries of the firm's area of service?

- Under what circumstances can the contract be transferred to another firm or state, and how does this affect guarantees?

- How does a change of beneficiary affect the contract?

- How much of the funds being paid to the firm will be deposited until the funeral is provided, and where will they be deposited?

- Who is responsible for paying taxes on income or interest generated? *Note that, in many cases, the funeral home earns the interest, while the beneficiaries pay the taxes.*[40]

- If the prices are not guaranteed, who is responsible for paying additional amounts, if any, that are due at the time of the funeral?

- Should the income or interest generated by invested preneed funds exceed future price increases in the selected funeral, who is entitled to the excess funds?

- Under what circumstances, if any, may the contract be cancelled, and how much of the funds paid to the firm will be refunded?

- What effect will missed or late payments have?

When you are done making the arrangements, the funeral provider must give you an itemized statement of the total cost of the goods and services you have selected. If the provider does not know the cost of the cash advance items at the time, he or she must give you a "good faith estimate" in writing.[41] This statement must also disclose any legal, cemetery, or crematory requirements that you purchase any specific goods or services.[42]

Once your arrangements have been made, prepare a list of prepaid items using the Prepaid Items form in Part 2. Insert *copies* of the funeral contract, general price list, statement of goods and services, and other pertinent documentation in your planner. Examples of prepaid items to include are the:

- casket

- plot

- grave marker

- chapel

- pastor

- announcements

- death certificates

This exercise will prevent the family from having to decipher the whole contract, which, as you will become aware, is quite lengthy.

More Questions to Ask

- *Does this state require a license or permit number to sell preneed funeral contracts? If so, what is your license number?*

- *What is the name, address, and telephone number of the enforcement agency in this state?* Every state except Alabama and District of Columbia has a controlling agency that regulates the sales of these contracts.

- *What does your funeral home offer, and are the items listed in the contract?*

- *Please explain the difference between the standard professional service fee and other services listed in the contract.*

- *What if we need the services of two funeral homes in two different states?*

- *What is the time limit to cancel this contract? What happens if we choose to cancel after the time limit has passed?*

- *What happens if the funeral home goes out of business or is sold?*

- *Regarding the funeral service, is there a choice of visitation hours? Can we select the time of the funeral?*

- *Are there other possible charges I need to know about, i.e., for the guest book, announcements, death certificates, thank you notes, etc.?* These are not prepaid items in most cases. FYI, Hallmark has an excellent selection of Thank You cards.

- *What documents are you going to need from me?* Fill these out at the preplanning appointment. This prevents having the family go to the funeral home at the time of expiration.

- *What caskets or urns do you offer?* Once the subject of caskets is discussed, the funeral home is required by the Federal Trade Commission (FTC) to provide you with a General Price List containing the current cost of individual goods and services offered. Note that this is a *price list*. It does not show the actual cost of the goods and services. Have them show you the caskets or urns they offer. Caskets are available in wood, aluminum, bronze, or other materials, and range in price from hundreds to thousands of dollars. Urns are available in wood, metal, ceramic, and cloisonné, and range from under $100 to over $1000. Both caskets and urns may be purchased at discount prices on the Internet. Again, prices vary widely, so shop around. Should you purchase your casket or urn from a funeral home, make sure it is written in the contract to save your loved ones from being pressured to upgrade.

• *What type of grave markers do you offer?* Grave markers come in different shapes and sizes. Most in Florida, where the authors live, are flat for grass-cutting purposes, but have a vase for flowers attached to the top. Be prepared to tell the funeral director what wording you want on the marker.

• *Can cemetery plots, columbarium niches or other cremation internment options (e.g., internment in a scattering garden) be purchased through your funeral home? Where are they located?* There are pros and cons to buying cemetery plots in advance. You may want the assurance of knowing your grave will be close to other family members. In this case, the longer you put off the purchase, the more likely it is that adjoining plots will be sold to someone else. On the other hand, many years may pass between the purchase date and your death. During this time, you or your family may move to another city and want to be buried there. You or your loved ones may decide you want to be cremated instead. The cemetery may change ownership and maintenance could decline. The neighborhood in which the cemetery is located could become less desirable. Keep in mind that when you purchase a lot, it is very difficult to sell. In any case, choose wisely. Generations to come will look for you, so make it easy for them.

- *Are there other plots available in the same location for burial of other family members (if desired)?*

- *Does the price include perpetual care and maintenance?*

- *Does the cemetery meet the requirements of my religion (if applicable)?*

- *What restrictions are placed on urns (if applicable), monuments and burial vaults?*

- *Are limousines available for the family at the visitation and funeral? Is this charge included in the package?*

- *Are police available if the need arises? If so, who pays for this service?*

- *What happens to the flowers after the funeral? Is there a charge to have them dropped off at a nursing home or other facility?*

Flowers

Traditionally, the family buys flowers for the casket, and selects the deceased's favorite flowers. If the casket will be open during the funeral service, the flowers should complement the clothing worn by the departed. Flowers can be very expensive.

Even though Mama had requested tea roses, I (Judy) chose long-stemmed pink roses because the designer told me that tiny tea roses would not be visible on Mama's coffin. She did, however, incorporate tea roses into her design to create a remarkable piece. The cost was over $300.

Some flowers on the coffin during the funeral service are placed on the grave after it is filled. Cemeteries allow very few flowers on the grave, so make arrangements in advance as to where the remainder of the flowers will go. After Mama's funeral was over, I gave some of the long-stemmed roses to family members and Mama's friends at the assisted living facility.

Video

When Mama passed, a huge snow storm was raging up north. Because the airports were closed, most of our family members and friends could not attend her funeral. I (Judy) had the bright idea that if one could hire a videographer for weddings, surely someone out there would shoot a funeral.

I called the local camera shop, which put me in touch with a highly competent videographer. I explained to the gentleman why I wanted him to videotape Mama's funeral—that severe weather precluded most people from attending— because I didn't want him to think I was nuts. When he expressed no reservations about my request and agreed to shoot it, I gave him specific instructions, namely that I wanted him to focus not on the bereaved, but on the minister and the speakers.

Per our arrangement, the videographer would shoot the funeral service only. But, because we were so caught up in Mama's funeral—a celebration of her life—he went along with us to the grave site. My nephew sang graveside, which everyone raved about for days afterward, so I was exuberant that it was caught on tape.

I sent video tapes up north to folks whom had missed the funeral. Because the videographer did such a terrific job, they actually felt like they were there. I was so grateful. It was like a made-for-TV movie.

Judy on Women's Clothing

It's a known fact that women are vain. It is also a known fact that there are parts of our bodies we want to hide, cover, cut off, get rid of, whatever. But, we always strive to make the best of what God has given us to work with. Sometimes, it "ain't much," and, as we get older, it seems like less and less.

At our funerals, we will be laid out for all to see and we want to look as good as we can. If we want, we can cover up all of our body parts except for our heads. We can wear long sleeves, high necks to cover our sagging skin, or close the coffin altogether. After all, it's our party. If the coffin will be closed, the funeral director and the advocates for death and dying will suggest the need for loved ones to see you for closure, so you'll still need to be prepared. Someone is going to check you out.

When you choose what you are wearing, wear what you like, cover up what you must, and don't forget costume jewelry. Earrings are a must for pierced ears: the holes have certainly grown with age. Underwear is optional. If you don't like it, don't wear it—just let it all hang loose.

Makeup is provided by the funeral home. Some makeup artists have more talent than others. Hope and pray that you get one whom graduated with honors. The same goes for the hair dresser. You will need a fairly recent photo of yourself for the funeral director, because those doing your makeup and hair will have no way of knowing what you looked like in life. You don't want to look slick if you've always been fluffy.

Don't forget your nails. In a prolonged illness, nails are usually ignored, and by the time you check out, they could have become claws. Pick a soft polish to complement your clothing.

Select a perfume that you really like, and have them spray you well. We all like to smell nice.

Have you thought about how you would like to have your hands displayed? They can be folded over your chest, or you can hold something, like a small Bible, a flower or a hankie. Just remember, it's your choice.

If the casket is to remain closed, do you want a picture of yourself on top of it? Your picture could be surrounded by flowers . . .

Finally, don't forget that your flowers and clothing should complement the casket lining, which comes in pastel blue, pink, ivory, and white.

Paul on Men's Clothing

Wear a dark suit. (What else is there for men to know?)

Step Three: Paying for Your Funeral

This section discusses the types of funding available to pay for your funeral. A detailed discussion of funding is outside the scope of this book. Besides, we must stress that *the authors are not certified financial planners.* Our purpose here is to let you know what types of funding exist, so that you may *seek expert advice.* In Part 3, Survivor's Guide to Dealing with Death, we offer insight for your loved ones who will have to handle insurance claims and medical bills that will arrive posthumously.

There are several types of funding available to pay for your funeral, including trusts, life insurance, savings accounts, and annuities.

A funeral home may place preplanning funds it receives in a funeral *trust fund* at a financial institution authorized by your state to receive trust deposits. Typically, those funds are invested in interest-bearing accounts. Interest earned usually stays in the account, although some states allow funeral homes to withdraw some or all of the interest. Some states also allow funeral homes to retain a percentage of the funds as an administrative fee.[43] In many cases, you will have to pay federal income tax on interest earned each year.[44] There also may be state tax liabilities associated with trust funding. Understand all the facts about trusts before you sign anything.

A better idea, however, may be to open a Totten Trust because, then, *you* control your money. A Totten Trust allows you to go to a bank and open a trust account by yourself. After you die, a Totten Trust can be paid out quickly to the funeral home with a minimum of formalities. Because the money transfers directly, there is no need for a third-party Trustee, and because the assets are in a trust, they are kept out of probate. You can revoke a Totten Trust at any time during your life. The beneficiary (in this case, the funeral home) can't take the money out until after you die.[45]

Life insurance policies are available that are tailored to prefund your funeral. These products earn interest, just like trusts, and many of these accounts are not taxable. They can also be set up to be excluded as an asset for state assistance, like Medicaid.[46] Upon your death, this type of life insurance policy directs payment of the death benefit to your funeral home. Not all states allow these policies. When considering this form of prefunding, inquire as to:

- How much life insurance must be purchased to secure a guaranteed price funeral?

- If the death benefit is adjusted for inflation or a flat amount?

- May you be disqualified for health reasons?

- Will the entire death benefit be paid, even if the total premiums have not been paid at time of death?

Again, make sure you understand everything before you sign anything.

Another option in prefunding your funeral is to open a *savings account* for that purpose at your local bank. This type of savings account, sometimes referred to as a payable-on-death-certificate (POD), is usually held in joint names: the funeral home's and yours[47]. Hence, when you die, the account automatically belongs to the funeral home. Though savings accounts do earn interest, the interest earned is subject to income tax. You'll need to consider whether the interest earned by the account will offset inflation and cover the future price of your funeral. Questions to ask:

- Will the funeral home guarantee the price of the funeral by agreeing to provide the funeral for the balance in the account?

- Is the family or estate responsible for the difference?

- Who is entitled to excess funds, the funeral home or the family?

Annuities, which provide periodic payments as retirement income, are more often used in a non-preneed environment. Normally, it is used as a way to tax-defer savings, but it may have a limited use in preneed funding.

A preneed annuity is paid out as a lump sum and, technically, is not a death benefit.[48] Again, get all the facts and understand before you sign.

Some people may receive survivor benefits under a state's Medicaid program, or from the Social Security Administration's Supplemental Security Income (SSI) program. When making your funding arrangement, ask what the impact will be on your funeral arrangement if you ever need to qualify for Medicaid or SSI.

DID YOU KNOW?

If you expire in a nursing home, hospital or assisted living facility, they will want your body removed as soon as possible because they always seem to need an extra bed. It is important that someone in the family knows which funeral home you are to be taken to. Ask the funeral home for several business cards and give them to family members.

GENERATIONS TO COME

Genealogy has become an obsession for some, a mere hobby for others. I (Judy) find it truly fascinating to learn about my relatives whom have passed. Often, though, I wish I could find more information.

I was the record keeper of my parents' lives. I found it to be interesting and educational. The first thing I did was purchase a trunk and a padlock with a key, because I found it easier to keep everything in one place for safekeeping.

I made a scrapbook containing sympathy cards the family received, the obituary from an out-of-town newspaper, copies of the eulogies, sprigs of special flowers, memory cards from the funeral guest book, etc. Items that went into the locker included:

- Scrap book

- Flag from Daddy's coffin (he was a veteran)

- World War II medals

- World War II military issue watch

- Daddy's map of the path he fought in World War II

- Letters he wrote from Europe to me when I was an infant

- Wallets and drivers licenses

- Thank you letter from the Holocaust Museum in Jerusalem, thanking Daddy for donating photographs of the liberation of Dachau (they also erected a plaque in his name)

- Letters or cards of my parents' siblings to capture their handwriting

- Pictures of my parents' siblings

- A photograph of Daddy teaching a class (he was a teacher early in his career)

- A piece of crystal belonging to my grandmother

- Original deed to my grandparents' home

- Newspaper clippings of "happenings" in the family

- Photos of my grandparents

- Other little things my parents thought were special, such as a guardian angel

- The family Bible

- The dresses Mama wore to my daughters' weddings

Remember, years after you have passed, someone will try to stitch your life together. Make it easy for him or her. Appoint a record keeper, someone from the family who is organized, and who neither keeps every scrap of paper nor throws everything away.

PART 2:

Your Funeral Plans: Forms

DID YOU KNOW?

It is wise to review and revise your plans every few years.

GENERAL INSTRUCTIONS

This part includes forms that you should include in your planner. You could conceivably complete them herein, though you likely won't have enough room. We suggest you use these forms to create forms suitable for your purposes, then include the completed forms in your planner. Don't forget, too, to include copies of your will, living will, and advance directives. See Figures 1, 2, and 3 in Part 1 for samples of a living will and advance directives suitable for residents of Florida. Remember, *it is imperative that you use forms required by your state*. Since this book contain invaluable information for your survivors, we suggest that you store a copy of it in your planner, as well.

Cover Letter

To my loved ones:

Enclosed in this planner are my desires following my death. I have taken great care to protect you and help you while you are grieving my passing. Copies of my will, living will, advance directives, and other legal documentation are contained in this book, and the location of the originals is noted. When my wishes are not legally binding, such as whom I want notified of my passing or whom I want as pallbearers, I have annotated them herein. In some cases, I may have jotted down special memories or notes to you. *Please*, follow the instructions in this planner carefully. Because I have taken such time and care, you'll know that this is what I truly wanted. Fulfilling my wishes will spare you from additional grief, and will show your true love and respect for me.

Love,

_____

(Signature)

_____

(Date)

Living Will

Declaration made this ___day of ____, 20__, I, _____, willfully and voluntarily make known my desire that my dying not be artificially prolonged under the circumstances set forth below, and I do hereby declare that, if at any time I am mentally or physically incapacitated

___(initial) and I have a terminal condition

or ___(initial) and I have an end-state condition

or ___(initial) and I am in a persistent vegetative state

and if my attending or treating physician and other consulting physician have determined that there is no reasonable medical probability of my recovery from such condition, I direct that life-prolonging procedures be withheld or withdrawn with the application of such procedures would serve only to prolong artificially the process of dying, and that I be permitted to die naturally with only the administration of medication or the performance of any medical procedure deemed necessarily to provide me with comfort care or to alleviate pain.

It is my intention that this declaration be honored by my family and physician as the final expression of my legal right to refuse medical or surgical treatment and to accept the consequences for such refusal.

In the event I have been determined to be unable to provide express and informed consent regarding the withholding, withdrawal, or continuation of life-prolonging procedures, I wish to designate, as my surrogate to carry out the provisions of this declaration:

Name:_____

Address:_____

_____Zip Code:_____

Phone:_____

I understand the full import of this declaration, and I am emotionally and mentally competent to make this declaration.

Additional instructions (optional):

_____

_____

_____

(Signed)

_____   _____
(Witness)   (Witness)

_____   _____
(Address)   (Address)

_____   _____
(Phone)   (Phone)

(At least one witness must be neither a spouse nor a blood relative of the signatory.)

DESIGNATION OF HEALTH CARE SURROGATE

Name:_____

    (Last Name)   *(First Name)*   *(Middle Initial)*

In the event that I have been determined to be incapacitated to provide informed consent for medical treatment and surgical and diagnostic procedures, I wish to designate as my surrogate for health care decisions:

Name: _____

Address:_____Zip Code: _____

Phone: _____

If my surrogate is unwilling or unable to perform his or her duties, I wish to designate as my alternate surrogate:

Name: _____

Address:_____Zip Code: _____

Phone: _____

I fully understand that this designation will permit my designee to make health care decisions and to provide, withhold, or withdraw consent on my behalf; to apply for public benefits to defray cost of health care; and to authorize my admission to or transfer from a health care facility.

Additional instructions (optional):

_____

_____

_____

_____

I further affirm that this designation is not being made a condition of treatment or admission to a health care facility. I will notify and send a copy of this document to the following persons other than my surrogate, so they may know who my surrogate is.

Name:_____

Name:_____

Signed:_____   Date:_____

Witnesses: 1._____

2._____

(At least one witness must be neither a spouse nor a blood relative of the signatory.)

FLORIDA
DO NOT RESUSCITATE ORDER

(Please use ink)

Patient's Full Legal Name_____   _____
(Print or Type Name)   (Date)

PATIENT'S STATEMENT

Based upon informed consent, I, the undersigned, hereby direct that CPR be withheld or withdrawn. **(If not signed by patient, check applicable box):**

☐ Surrogate   ☐ Proxy (both as defined in Chapter 765, F. S.)

☐ Court appointed guardian ☐ Durable power of attorney (pursuant to Chapter 709, F. S.)

_____

(Applicable Signature)   (Print or Type Name)

PHYSICIAN'S STATEMENT

I, the undersigned, a physician licensed pursuant to Chapter 458 or 459, F. S., am the physician of the patient named above. I hereby direct the withholding or withdrawing of cardiopulmonary resuscitation (artificial ventilation, cardiac compression, endotracheal intubation, and defibrillation) from the patient in the event of the patient's cardiac or respiratory arrest.

_____

(Signature of Physician)   (Date)   Telephone Number (Emergency)

_____

(Print or Type Name)   (Physician's Medical License Number)

Pursuant to s.401.45, F. S., a copy or original of this DNRO may be honored by hospital emergency services, nursing homes, assisted living facilities, home health agencies, hospices, adult family-care, and emergency medical services.

NOTIFICATION LIST INSTRUCTIONS

Use the Notification List to compile names, addresses, and phone numbers of relatives and friends you want notified in the event of your death. Addresses are important for thank you notes after the funeral, and for sending memory cards to those whom are unable to attend. The calling list can be prioritized and divided among loved ones. Select family members and close friends for this task.

NOTIFICATION LIST

Dear loved ones:

When I have passed, please notify my dear family and friends listed on the following pages. Please call first in order of priority those who have been prioritized, then all others whom have not. When applicable, I have made notations in regard to specific people, such as whom I would prefer to call them or a special message from me I would like passed to them. I would like _____ to be in charge of completing this Notification list. Thank you for your time and effort.

     *   *   *

NAME:_____

ADDRESS:_____

TELEPHONE:_____

RELATIONSHIP:_____

PRIORITY:_____

NAME:_____

ADDRESS:_____

TELEPHONE:_____

RELATIONSHIP:_____

PRIORITY:_____

NAME:_____

ADDRESS:_____

TELEPHONE:_____

RELATIONSHIP:_____

PRIORITY:_____

NAME:_____

ADDRESS:_____

TELEPHONE:_____

RELATIONSHIP:_____

PRIORITY:_____

NAME:_____

ADDRESS:_____

TELEPHONE:_____

RELATIONSHIP:_____

PRIORITY:_____

NAME:_____

ADDRESS:_____

TELEPHONE:_____

RELATIONSHIP:_____

PRIORITY:_____

NAME:_____

ADDRESS:_____

TELEPHONE:_____

RELATIONSHIP:_____

PRIORITY:_____

NAME:_____

ADDRESS:_____

TELEPHONE:_____

RELATIONSHIP:_____

PRIORITY:_____

NAME:_____

ADDRESS:_____

TELEPHONE:_____

RELATIONSHIP:_____

PRIORITY:_____

NAME:_____

ADDRESS:_____

TELEPHONE:_____

RELATIONSHIP:_____

PRIORITY:_____

NAME:_____

ADDRESS:_____

TELEPHONE:_____

RELATIONSHIP:_____

PRIORITY:_____

FUNERAL WISHES

OF

_____
(Name)

_____
(City, State, and Zip Code)

Dated this _____ day of _____, 20____

- Pastor/Rabbi:_____

- Church/Synagogue:_____

- Music Type:_____

- Special Selections:_____

_____

_____

Vocalist:_____

- Eulogies (I would like the following people to speak at my service):

  1.＿＿＿＿＿＿＿＿＿＿＿＿＿＿＿＿＿＿＿＿＿＿＿＿＿＿＿＿＿＿

  2.＿＿＿＿＿＿＿＿＿＿＿＿＿＿＿＿＿＿＿＿＿＿＿＿＿＿＿＿＿＿

  3.＿＿＿＿＿＿＿＿＿＿＿＿＿＿＿＿＿＿＿＿＿＿＿＿＿＿＿＿＿＿

  4.＿＿＿＿＿＿＿＿＿＿＿＿＿＿＿＿＿＿＿＿＿＿＿＿＿＿＿＿＿＿

  5.＿＿＿＿＿＿＿＿＿＿＿＿＿＿＿＿＿＿＿＿＿＿＿＿＿＿＿＿＿＿

- Pallbearers:

  1.＿＿＿＿＿＿＿＿＿＿＿＿＿＿＿＿＿＿＿＿＿＿＿＿＿＿＿＿＿＿

  2.＿＿＿＿＿＿＿＿＿＿＿＿＿＿＿＿＿＿＿＿＿＿＿＿＿＿＿＿＿＿

  3.＿＿＿＿＿＿＿＿＿＿＿＿＿＿＿＿＿＿＿＿＿＿＿＿＿＿＿＿＿＿

  4.＿＿＿＿＿＿＿＿＿＿＿＿＿＿＿＿＿＿＿＿＿＿＿＿＿＿＿＿＿＿

  5.＿＿＿＿＿＿＿＿＿＿＿＿＿＿＿＿＿＿＿＿＿＿＿＿＿＿＿＿＿＿

  6.＿＿＿＿＿＿＿＿＿＿＿＿＿＿＿＿＿＿＿＿＿＿＿＿＿＿＿＿＿＿

- The type of service I prefer:

  ☐　Traditional

  ☐　Contemporary

  ☐　Celebration of Life

  ☐　Memorial Service

- My preferences for flowers:_____
_____
_____

- During my funeral, I want to be dressed in:_____
_____
_____
_____

- I DO /DO NOT want a receiving line. (circle one)
- I DO/DO NOT want flowers given to the ladies at the funeral. (circle one)

Prepaid Burial Items List

Dear loved ones:

The following items have already been paid for. These items are specified in the funeral contract, but are listed here for your convenience. Please see the funeral contract for specific details.

ITEM:

☐ Transportation

☐ Burial

☐ Grave plot   Location:_____

☐ Grave liner

☐ Grave marker

☐ Casket   Model/Material:_____

☐ Casket liner   Material:_____

☐ Embalming

☐ Makeup

☐ Hair

☐ Funeral service

☐ Chapel   Name/Location:_____

☐ Pastor/Rabbi   Name/Telephone:_____

☐ Flowers   Details/Quantities:_____

_____

_____

_____

☐ Limousine(s)   Style/Quantity:_____

☐ Photographer: Name/Telephone:_____

☐ Videographer: Name/Telephone:_____

☐ Guest book   Style:_____

☐ Invitations   Style/Quantity:_____

☐ Thank you cards   Style/Quantity:_____

☐ Death Certificates Quantity:_____

☐ _____

☐ _____

☐ _____

☐ _____

☐ _____

☐ _____

☐ _____

☐ _____

☐ _____

PREPAID CREMATION ITEMS LIST

Dear loved ones:

The following items have already been paid for. These items are specified in the funeral contract, but are listed here for your convenience. Please see the funeral contract for specific details.

☐ Cremation

☐ Funeral Service

☐ Memorial Service

☐ Pastor/Rabbi   Name/Telephone:_____

☐ Urn   Style/Material:_____

☐ Keepsake Urn   Style/Quantity:_____

☐ Keepsake Jewelry   Style/Quantity:_____

☐ Memorial Tablet(s)   Style/Quantity:_____

☐ Columbarium Niche   Location:_____

☐ Urn Garden   Location:_____

☐ Scattering Garden   Location:_____

☐ Guest book   Style:_____

☐ Invitations   Style/Quantity:_____

☐ Thank you cards   Style/Quantity:_____

☐ Death Certificates: Quantity:_____

Documentation List

Copies of the following legal or financial documents are enclosed herein:

☐ Living Will

☐ Designation of Health Care Surrogate

☐ Do-Not-Resuscitate Order

☐ Last Will and Testament

☐ Funeral Contract

☐ Financial Documents

☐ Life Insurance Policies (Policy Nos._____)

☐ _____

☐ _____

Originals are located at:_____

_____

_____

People whom have copies are:

NAME:_____

ADDRESS:_____

TELEPHONE:_____

RELATIONSHIP:_____

NAME:_____

ADDRESS:_____

TELEPHONE:_____

RELATIONSHIP:_____

BUSINESS CARD HOLDER

Include in your planner a business card holder with the following professionals' cards inserted:

Attorney	Financial Consultant
Pastor	Bank Representative
Insurance Agent	Funeral Director

LIST OF FINANCIAL ACCOUNTS

ACCOUNT # _____

Account Type: _____

Financial Institution: _____

Address: _____

_____

Account Status: _____

ACCOUNT # _____

Account Type: _____

Financial Institution: _____

Address: _____

_____

Account Status: _____

ACCOUNT # _____

Account Type: _____

Financial Institution: _____

Address: _____

_____

Account Status: _____

ACCOUNT # _____

Account Type: _____

Financial Institution: _____

Address: _____

_____

Account Status: _____

ACCOUNT # _____

Account Type: _____

Financial Institution: _____

Address: _____

_____

Account Status: _____

ACCOUNT # _____

Account Type: _____

Financial Institution: _____

Address: _____

_____

Account Status: _____

Special Gifts

To my loved ones:

I would like the following items to be distributed accordingly:

GIFT: RECIPIENT:

_____

_____

_____

_____

_____

_____

_____

_____

_____

_____

_____

SPECIAL NOTES AND MEMORIES

DID YOU KNOW?

It's not a good idea to put the only copy of your preferences in a safe deposit box. You may die on a weekend or holiday, or holiday weekend like both of Judy's parents did, and your family may have to make arrangements before the box can be opened.

PART 3:

Survivors' Guide to Dealing with Death

YOUR LOVED ONE HAS DIED...
NOW WHAT?

☐ Call 911 if your loved one passes at home. Call the hospice provider if your loved one was under hospice care. (Hospice Provider:_____). *The body will be transferred to the funeral home noted herein. In some cases, the police may have the body taken to the county coroner or medical examiner to determine the cause of death. In any case, a physician will determine the cause of death and sign the death certificate.*

☐ Get several copies of the death certificate.

☐ Complete the Notification List in Part 2.

☐ Immediately notify banks, credit card companies, etc., that the account holder is deceased. Request in writing that all accounts be frozen until an executor is appointed. Include a copy of the death certificate and reference the relevant account number with each request.

☐ Notify the Social Security Administration

☐ Arrange with the funeral home the services accompanying the disposition of the remains. Your loved one preplanned his or her funeral and his or her wishes are documented herein. Copies of everything you will need should be contained in this planner. The location of original documents should also be noted herein.

DID YOU KNOW?

Publishing an obituary in a newspaper puts you at risk of burglary. Criminals who read obituaries may look in the phone book for your address, then burglarize your home.

DEALING WITH GRIEF

Psychologists have determined that there are five stages of grieving. They are:

- denial and isolation

- anger

- bargaining

- depression

- acceptance[49]

Though the knowledge of these stages of grieving certainly won't ease your pain, it will help to understand these stages because you can identify why you're feeling the way you are, and why others are feeling the way they are. It also helps to understand that your feelings are *normal*.

Not everyone goes through these stages of grieving in the expected order, though, because no one grieves the same. This is critically important, especially when you are dealing with close friends and family members. Just because someone doesn't seem as devastated as you are doesn't mean he or she didn't love or care for your loved one as much as you did. Others may be in different phases of grieving than you are.

In fact, because you likely won't be going through the grieving process solo, and others may not be in the same stage of grief as you are, you will be required to help your loved ones get a grip. We offer some insight below in identifying the stages of grief, and helping others get through them.

The *denial and isolation* stage typically is the first stage the bereaved go through, but not always.[50] Those in the denial stage might avoid family and friends, refuse to return phone calls, avoid talking about the deceased, or blame the doctor or hospital for screwing up. Ways to help people suffering through the denial stage are to be nonjudgmental of their behavior and to not take anything personally. Be a good listener if they want to talk.

In the *anger* stage, the bereaved ask "Why me?" They feel angry that their loved one has died while others are allowed to live, and may become angry with God. This is also the stage in which people accuse family members and friends of uncaring attitudes.[51] The anger can be intense, and can alienate family and friends. Be aware that dealing with others in this stage may bring on anger in yourself.

Ways to be helpful during this stage are to remember that the anger is not directed at you, but at the situation. Recognize the anger as resulting from the grieving process and do not allow it to alienate you from family members or friends. Also, give yourself a break. Spend time away from people suffering through this stage, but assure them you are not deserting them.

Once the bereaved have vented their anger at loved ones—and God—they enter the *bargaining* phase.[52] In this phase, they attempt to come to some agreement in which they make promises to God to change their lives or decide to do something special before they, themselves, suffer disability or death. Promises made in this stage may be resulting from guilt. As is helpful in every stage, be a good listener to someone in this stage. Allow the grieving person to express their feelings—to get it all out.

After the bargaining phase, the bereaved usually enter a *depression* stage.[53] This is the beginning of realization that a loved one has died. Depression may be exacerbated by financial difficulties, loss of independence, and loss of intimacy that occur from the loss of a spouse or loved one. This stage of grief tends to be a quiet one.

Your first reaction in caring for someone in this stage may be to try to cheer them up. Realize, though, that a grieving person may find more comfort in talking about his or her feelings. Your presence may be all that is necessary. Again, the best way to help someone in this stage is to be a good listener. Just sit and *listen.*

Acceptance is considered the final stage of grief.[54] This as a time of resolution for the bereaved. Hope emerges and one might feel that the good days start outnumbering the bad, which can be a double-edged sword because, sometimes, guilt may result from feeling happy. Those in this final stage will find their senses of humor again, as daily life begins to return to normal.

Now that the "formal" stages of grief have been delineated, understand that within any of those stages, the bereaved may —often at the same time—experience:

• Shock

• Anger

• Physical problems

• Fear

• Panic

• Regret

• Loneliness

• Depression

• Personal growth[55]

When my (Paul's) mother passed away, my oldest brother Greg (who was closest to Mom) and I shared tears over Mom's passing, yet my brother Mark cried openly only once that I noticed while I was in Phoenix. Now, if I hadn't understood the grieving process from previous undergraduate psychology classes, it would have been easy to become infuriated with him. It could have been easy to blame him for not caring, or for not loving Mom as much as we did. Don't let that happen to you. Uncle Bob may still be in shock or he might be in denial. He may be attempting to be "strong" for the rest of the family, while in private he is sobbing uncontrollably. Don't assume anything.

Time will pass but the grief won't, at least not soon. Experts vary on the duration of grief, but a year-and-a-half is still considered normal.

I (Paul) was a sales representative at the time of my mom's passing. Death can be especially detrimental to a sales rep's job performance. A successful sales rep, like an athlete, spends a significant amount of time motivating himself, getting himself in the right mental framework, "pumping up" his positive attitude. Frankly, to me this was impossible for the longest time. Because of this, my sales performance plummeted. The problem with grief is, you never know when it's going to hit you. For me, even months after Mom's passing, grief always hit me at the most inopportune time: five minutes before an important sales call. There were many prospects, I'm certain, whom were curious as to why my eyes were red: Had I been crying and, if so, why? Or had I decided to smoke a little weed to ease my nerves before this critical presentation? What was disconcerting was that I could "see" them wondering. I knew that, unless they had lost a loved one, they wouldn't understand that my fresh tears were for someone I had lost eight months ago, because our culture expects us to get over it and get on with life in two or three months. In any case, it left me feeling unconfident and vulnerable.

You, too, will feel vulnerable after your loved one's death. Beware. It's not just a feeling. If you are not careful, someone may take advantage of you.

Due to the short time I would be in Phoenix after Mom's passing, my brothers and I decided the fastest way to sell her belongings was to have a yard sale. So, we placed an ad in the classifieds.

On Saturday morning, the day of the yard sale, we arrived at Mom's house at five a.m. It was still an hour before daybreak and—can you believe those yard salers?—there was a lady in a black Mercedes, waiting for us to bring out the goods.

As we hauled out Mom's furniture and personal belongings, we spoke with the kind, middle-aged, and obviously affluent woman. We told her the reason for the yard sale was that our mom had passed away just days ago. Of course, she sympathized with our tragedy.

As we continued to lug out furniture, she carefully picked through Mom's belongings. Finally, she purchased something inexpensive and was on her way.

Less than an hour later—before our next visitor arrived—we realized that the kind lady had stolen Mom's jewelry box, full of expensive jewelry!

When dealing with illnesses of long duration, bereavement may begin *before* a loved one dies. This is called *anticipatory grief.* Anticipatory grief does not eliminate post-death grieving.[56] In my (Judy's) case, this is exactly what occurred.

Mama was the bravest person I have ever had the pleasure of knowing. Her life was plagued with medical maladies of many kinds, but she was an accepting person with a great sense of humor, a spirit of argument and a strong determination to overcome. She was a feisty little old lady whom thought like and acted as if she were 30.

My grieving began in February, 1999, when I received an emergency phone call from Mama's next-door neighbor. Apparently, Mama had gone out to the mailbox to get the mail, when she tripped over a pothole and fell. The Emergency Room nurse tried to clean up the abrasions, but Mama had gravel and dirt embedded in her forehead and knees. Eight hours later, we left the ER with no diagnosis other than a broken nose.

A week later, she was back in the hospital again. Mama had come down with the flu, which caused a bad case of pneumonia. The doctors determined that, because of her fall, she had lost an extreme amount of blood internally, and her blood count was seven—half of what is medically acceptable in a patient.

After several blood transfusions she began to improve. The gravel in her forehead came to the surface, and had to be removed. After a 30-day stay at the hospital, she was back at my house for recuperation. Unfortunately, this was just the beginning: from the time she fell until the time she passed, she was admitted into the hospital about 20 times.

During one hospital stay, she was to be admitted to a nursing home to undergo physical therapy. I asked the nurse to remove the pik line—which are used with patients whom have no veins capable of handling blood draws or transfusions—because her intravenous medication had been discontinued. The nurse removed the line, but, when doing so, neglected to apply enough pressure. When Mama asked me why her hair was so wet, I had great difficulty telling her that she was soaked in blood, that more transfusions were inevitable. Though our local hospital is rated within the top 100 in the nation, I was afraid its staff would finish Mama off during her stay.

At Christmas she was in the hospital again, this time for a month. I decorated a tree and brought tons of presents. The entire family came, sharing gifts and love. We had our own "Hospital Christmas," complete with a traditional prime rib dinner from my kitchen with all the fixin's.

During another visit, when Mama had surgery for a colon resection, she contracted methicillin resistant staphylococcus aureus, or MRSA, in the operative site. This, of course, went unnoticed until I was helping her get dressed to go home, and discovered that her abdomen had turned deep red. I refused to take her home until the doctor saw her. He was paged back to the hospital, and decided to keep her longer.

In between hospital stays, Mama tried to put her life back in order, but it was becoming frightfully clear that she could no longer live alone. I suggested a nursing home, to which she violently opposed. "No, no, please no," she kept saying. I discussed this with my family. What were we going to do? Putting Mama in a nursing home would be defying her in a most horrible way.

I was tired of the whole mess. It was plaguing my conscience. Free time didn't exist: I was either at work or taking care of Mama. I was ignoring my family. I had no time for my husband, Shelby. Guilt was creeping into my bones.

When April came, Mama was in the hospital again when it became clear that she needed skilled care. Mama sat in her reclining chair, dressed in a cute yellow outfit. She watched as we packed her belongings, saying nothing. If her silent tears didn't speak for themselves, then everyone in the room must have been deaf.

We got her a private room, hoping that it would make the adjustment easier on her. We were wrong. A week or two into her stay at the nursing home, a nurse made a major goof: she withheld for an entire week medication that was used to increase Mama's red blood cells. When her blood count fell, she was transferred back to the hospital to undergo yet another blood transfusion, which at this count numbered over 20. Mama's long-term nursing home care lasted all of three weeks.

Over the next six months, Mama was in and out of the hospital. Because she was terminally ill, the nurses suggested I call hospice for an evaluation. Hospice provides comfort and support to terminally ill patients and their families, its goal being to improve the quality of the remainder of the patient's life. From hospice, I learned that the patient decides when to end medical treatment. Hospice offers bereavement and counseling services to families before and after a patient's death. Hospice also deals with the emotional, social and spiritual impact on family and friends.[57]

After having many questions answered, I made an appointment for Mama with the hospice nurse, but before the hospice nurse arrived, I had to tell Mama she was dying. I didn't want to be the one to tell her, but I didn't want someone else to tell her either.

Shelby met me at the nursing home. Mama and he were good buddies so it only seemed natural to have Shelby there, but what a burden to put on him.

Mama's eyes lit up, seeing us both there during the middle of the day. She insisted on getting out of bed to sit in her chair. We told her that we needed to talk to her. She knew what we had to say, though, before we ever said a word. We told her that we had been advised by her physician that her medication was no longer working and that she was dying. Had I not made her a promise long ago to not keep secrets, I doubt that I would have had the nerve to tell her, but as hard as it was, I had to honor my promise.

After we told her, we held her and we all cried together. It was one of the most difficult things I have ever had to do. I thought my heart would break, because Mama was not crying for herself: she was crying for *us*. She was ready to die, but she was worried about what would happen to us when she was gone.

After many more months of hospital stays and blood transfusions, we found ourselves having another hospital Christmas with Mama, just like the year before. This year, all the presents, rather than being wrapped in boxes, were in bags so that Mama could easily open them. We all knew that this would be Mama's last Christmas on earth. The strong-spirited family that we are, we put our feelings aside for the time being, and concentrated solely on making her Christmas a special one. No hospital food for Mama that day, only tender prime rib, twice-stuffed potatoes, and the works.

Our time with Mama in her hospital room that Christmas was the epitome of love in all its splendor, with hugs and kisses all around. It should have been an Oscar-winning performance, because when we left the hospital, we all sobbed. Were we all ready for the inevitable? No.

I made the best of my last day with her. We talked "girl talk," and I polished her nails. I made her milkshakes and tried to keep her mind off the pain. Shelby and my son came to visit in the afternoon, and when my son and I left the room to take a much-needed break, Mama told Shelby that her mother (who had died more than 60 years before) had come to take her away. Mama told Shelby that she was not ready to go, so she had sent Grandma away.

When I returned to her room, Mama told me that Daddy (whom had passed) was standing by her bed. She had dinner and another milkshake. I tucked her in bed, kissed her goodnight, and told her I would be back first thing in the morning. I never got the chance. Mama passed at 6:15 a.m. the following morning. It was the 31st of December.

Because my bereavement started long before she died, Mama's passing brought a great deal of comfort to me. Knowing that she is with those whom she had loved and lost gives me hope that, when it is my time to go, Mama will come to take me home.

When grieving, be patient with yourself. Give yourself time to move through the stages at your own pace, in your own way. Resist the temptation to suppress your feelings about the loss. Instead, cry when you need to cry and be angry when you need to be angry. Talk about your feelings with those who can console you. Laughter is a safety valve, so know that it's okay to laugh. Nurturing yourself physically, emotionally and spiritually will greatly facilitate your healing.

DEALING WITH PROBATE

Probate is the legal process that takes place after someone dies. Since probate rarely benefits beneficiaries, hopefully your loved one, with the help of a financial consultant or estate planning attorney (see the business card holder) took adequate steps to avoid it. However, if probate is a requirement, the following explanation will help you understand what probate entails.

Typically, probate involves attorneys.[58] Attorneys and court fees are paid from estate property, which otherwise would go to beneficiaries.[59] It usually works like this:

After one dies, the person named in the will as executor—or without a will, a person appointed by the judge—will file papers in local probate court. The executor proves the validity of the will, and presents the court with a list of property, debts, and beneficiaries. Relatives and creditors are officially notified of the decedent's death.[60]

During the probate process, which commonly takes a year, the executor must find, secure and manage the decedent's assets. Eventually, the court will authorize the executor to sell off assets to pay debts and taxes, and divide the rest among the beneficiaries named in the will.[61]

Not all property has to go through probate. Most states allow a certain amount of property to pass free of probate, and property that passes outside of a will, e.g., through a living trust, is not subject to probate.[62]

Because probate is a legal process that involves attorneys, court appearances, and differing state laws, it is outside the scope of this book. Our intent here is to briefly describe what probate is and what it involves. If you are involved in probate, seek legal counsel.

DID YOU KNOW?

To inherit property, you will need death certificates for both parents if they are listed on the deed and both are deceased.

DEALING WITH MEDICAL BILLS & INSURANCE CLAIMS

In most cases, after a loved one passes, the family is inundated with bills from hospitals, physicians and other medical ancillaries. These statements are often very hard to decipher. Some families find this task overwhelming, and would rather not deal with it at all. Let us warn you that this job is not going to go away by itself.

It is a known fact in the medical community that insurance companies will use all sorts of excuses to keep from paying claims. This keeps their bottom lines healthy.

[Author's note: Paul's wife has a lucrative sales career with a major health insurance company. Because that company has been very generous to Paul's wife and to Paul, himself, Paul thinks that health insurance companies are, oh, so great, and has distanced himself from Judy's propaganda. "Your wife works for the enemy," Judy has been known to grumble at him.]

One common excuse for not paying claims is they cannot identify you as their insured. This happens because they drop the last two digits of your Social Security Number, so that your claim is denied on the first pass. Another common tactic uses diagnosis codes. If you don't have a disease they won't pay, how do you know whether you have a disease if they disallow your test? As owner of a medical laboratory, my (Judy's) favorite denial is one based on medical necessity, where some $8.00 per hour employee with the insurance company is telling my physician that he cannot order a procedure because they feel it is medically unnecessary. Give me a break!

Claims are also denied by insurance companies due to overutilization. Overutilization occurs when insurance companies feel that a physician orders a test or procedure too often.

Our advice is to read the policy, then re-read it. If you still don't understand it, call the carrier. If, after talking to a customer service representative, you still have questions—call again. It has been my (Judy's) experience that if I call five people with the same question on the same day, I will receive five different answers.

With claims, there is a statute of limitations. If you don't get the claim paid and closed within one year, the insurance carrier legally may refuse to pay. If that happens, the burden falls on the patient, or, in the case of death, the executor of the estate.

A *Summary Notice*, more commonly called an *Explanation of Benefits (EOB)*, is mailed to a patient after any claim is submitted to Medicare. It contains the following information:

- Patient's name, address and Medicare Number

- Claim number

- Name of physician, hospital or ancillary providing service

- Phone number you can call to obtain answers to your questions

- Date of service

- Service provided

- Amount charged

- Amount Medicare approved

- Amount Medicare paid the provider

- Amount you may be billed

There may be more than one service listed on the EOB. If you do not understand this complex form, by all means call Medicare. The provider that provides the service deserves to be paid. It is your responsibility to help make that happen.

After a claim is filed with an insurance company, the carrier also mails you an EOB. An insurance company EOB contains the following information:

- Insured's name and address

- Date claim was processed

- Contract Number

- Group Number

- Provider of service

- Date of service

- Type of service

- Amount charged—the amount the provider charged the insurance company

- Allowed payment—the amount the insurance company will pay, but some of the allowed amount will go toward the deductible or coinsurance

- Deductible—the amount you must meet on an annual basis (check the policy for this amount)

- Coinsurance—the amount the patient is required to pay per the policy

- Payment amount—the amount that represents the maximum allowed by your contract

- Remarks—the reason the entire claim amount was not paid

- Patient Responsibility—the amount of the claim that the patient is required to pay

DEALING WITH SURVIVOR BENEFITS

Survivors may be eligible for benefits from the Social Security Administration or Veterans Administration. Benefits that may be available to you are briefly discussed below. Please note that benefits change from time to time. To insure this information is current, or if you feel you may be eligible for survivor benefits, contact the relevant agencies by phone or in writing.

Social Security Administration Benefits

If your loved one earned enough credits while he or she was working, you may be eligible for benefits under the Social Security Administration's Supplemental Security Income (SSI) program. You may contact the Social Security Administration by calling (800) 772-1213 or by visiting its website at http://www.ssa.gov.

Who is Eligible?

You can collect benefits if you are:

- A widow or widower who is 60 or older;

- A widow or widower who is 50 or older and disabled;

- A widow or widower of any age if you are caring for a child under the age of 16;

- A widow or widower of any age if you are caring for a disabled child who is receiving Social Security benefits.[63]

Children of the deceased can collect benefits if they are:

- Unmarried and under the age of 18;

- Under the age of 19, but in an elementary or secondary school as a full-time student;

- Age 18 or older and severely disabled, if the disability started before age 22.[64]

Parents can collect if they were dependent on the deceased for at least half of their support.[65]

Even if the deceased had remarried, divorced widows and widowers are eligible for benefits on the deceased's record. In order to qualify, they must:

- Be at least 60 years old (50 if disabled) and have been married to the deceased for at least 10 years;

- Be any age caring for a child who is eligible on the deceased's record;

- Not be eligible for an equal or higher benefit on his or her own record; and,

- Not be currently married, unless the marriage occurred after age 60 (50 for disabled widows).[66]

Special One-Time Death Benefit

If the deceased had enough credits, a special one-time death benefit of $255 can be paid only to a widow or widower, or minor children.[67]

Veterans Administration (VA) Benefits

If your loved one served in the armed forces, he or she may be eligible for certain benefits provided by the Veterans Administration (VA). All veterans, as well as their spouses and dependent children, are entitled to a free burial and grave marker, free-of-charge, in a national cemetery (the family is responsible for some expenses, such as transportation to the cemetery).[68] Some Public Service personnel and some civilians whom have provided military-related service are also eligible.[69] The FTC offers the following excellent advice:

> Beware of commercial cemeteries that advertise so-called "veterans' specials." These cemeteries sometimes offer a free plot for the veteran, but charge exorbitant rates for an adjoining plot for the spouse, as well as high fees for opening and closing each grave. Evaluate the bottom-line cost to be sure the special is as special as you may be led to believe.[70]

For more information visit the Department of Veterans Affairs website at http://www.cem.va.gov, or call (800) 827-1000 to reach the VA office in your area.

Who is Eligible?

A veteran may be eligible for a VA burial allowance if:

- He or she paid for it

  and

- You have not been reimbursed by another government agency or some other source, such as the deceased veteran's employer

  and

- The veteran was not discharged dishonorably.[71]

In order to be eligible, at least one of the following conditions must also be met:

- The veteran died due to a service-related disability

  or

- The veteran was getting a VA pension at the time of death

  or

- The veteran was entitled to receive a VA pension or compensation, but opted not to reduce his or her military retirement or disability pay

  or

- The veteran died in a VA hospital or while in a nursing home under a VA contract.[72]

How Much Can I Receive?

For a *service-related death,* the Veteran's Administration may pay up to $1500 toward burial expenses. Some or all of the costs of transferring the veteran may be reimbursed if he or she is buried in the VA national cemetery.[73]

For a *non-service-related death,* the VA may pay up to $300 toward burial and funeral expenses, and a $150 internment allowance. The cost of transferring the veteran may be reimbursed if he or she died while in a VA hospital or in a contracted nursing home.[74]

How Do I Apply?

Fill out VA Form 21-530, Application for Burial Allowance, available from the VA or your state's Department of Veterans Affairs. The funeral director can help you fill out this form if it is not already completed and contained herein. The VA will also need a DD214 (proof of the veteran's military service), a death certificate, and copies of funeral bills you have paid.

APPENDICES

AUTHORS' NOTE: While we have attempted in this book to provide you with information that will help you plan your passing, we would never recommend that you base your decisions on only one source of information. *It is critical that you become an informed consumer.* As we have reiterated time and again, *do your homework.* In the Appendices, we have provided additional information that will assist you in your efforts.

Appendix A is a glossary that provides thorough definitions and explanations of terms used in this book.

Appendix B is a list of websites we have found useful or interesting in our research. *In no way are the authors of this book in any way affiliated with the publishers of the websites listed, nor do we recommend one site over another, especially where providers of services and/or merchandise are concerned.* The Internet is too immense to list all of the websites available; those listed in Appendix B are simply ones that we found. Our purpose for listing them is solely to give you an idea of what's out there, and to provide you with resources for further research. Those websites, of course, may lead you to other sites you may find useful.

Appendix C is a list of state licensing boards that regulate the funeral industry. Call or write the licensing board in your state to ensure that those with whom you are planning to do business are licensed.

APPENDIX A:
GLOSSARY

Alternative Container

An unfinished wood box or other non-metal receptacle without ornamentation.

Advance Directive

An oral or written statement, witnessed in advance of serious illness or injury, that specifies what kind of treatment you want under serious medical conditions, or names someone to make those decisions for you.

Anticipatory Grief

When dealing with illnesses of long duration, bereavement that begins *before* a loved one dies. Anticipatory grief does not eliminate post-death grieving.

Basic Services Fee

The funeral home's cost of doing business. Defined by the Federal Trade Commission (FTC) as allowable coverage for the basic services of the funeral director and staff, furnished by the funeral provider in arranging any funeral, such as conducting the arrangements conference, planning the funeral, obtaining necessary permits, and placing obituary notices. It is the only funeral provider fee permitted for services, facilities, or unallocated overhead. It is nondeclinable, unless otherwise permitted by law. Also known as the Professional Services Fee.

Cash Advance Items Goods and services obtained from a third party by a funeral home.

Celebration-of-Life Funeral A funeral that celebrates the life of a loved one, rather than emphasizing grief over his or her passing.

Columbarium An indoor or outdoor wall containing niches. A columbarium may be a whole building, a room, a single wall, or a series of halls in a mausoleum or chapel.

Cremains Cremated remains; the ashes and bone fragments that remain after cremation is complete.

Cremation A process that reduces the body and its container to ashes and fragments by applying intense heat.

Direct Burial The body is buried shortly after death, usually in a simple container. No viewing or visitation is involved—no embalming is necessary—though a memorial service may be held.[75] Usually less expensive than a traditional, full-service funeral.

Direct Cremation

The body is cremated shortly after death, without embalming. No viewing or visitation is involved, though a memorial service may be held.[76]

Disposition

"The placement of cremated or whole remains in their final resting place."[77]

Do-Not-Resuscitate Order (DNR)

An advance directive that is placed in your medical chart, directing physicians and hospital staff to not resuscitate you in the event your heart or breathing stops. Some patients decide they would benefit from one in the case of terminal illness, e.g. Also known as a DNR.

Durable Power of Attorney for Health Care

An advance directive naming another person as your agent or proxy to make medical decisions for you, if you should become unable to make them for yourself. It becomes active any time you are unconscious or are unable to make medical decisions. Also known as Health Care Power of Attorney, Health Care Proxy, and Health Care Surrogate Designation.

Endowment Care Fund

"Money collected from cemetery property purchasers and placed in trust for the maintenance and upkeep of the cemetery."[78]

Entombment	Burial in a mausoleum.
Eulogy	A speech of praise given after someone has died.
Executor	"The person appointed to administer the estate of a person who has died leaving a will which nominates that person. Unless there is a valid objection, the judge will appoint the person named in the will to be executor. The executor must insure that the person's desires expressed in the will are carried out. Practical responsibilities include gathering up and protecting the assets of the estate, obtaining information in regard to all beneficiaries named in the will and any other potential heirs, collecting and arranging for payment of debts of the estate, approving or disapproving creditor's claims, making sure estate taxes are calculated, forms filed and tax payments made, and in all ways assisting the attorney for the estate (which the executor can select)."[79]
Explanation of Benefits (EOB)	A statement mailed to a patient after a claim has been submitted to an insurance carrier or Medicare. It contains such information as the claim number, service provided, physician's name, amount charged, etc.

General Price List	A list containing the current cost of, and disclosures about, individual goods and services offered. The Federal Trade Commission (FTC) requires funeral homes to provide you with a general price list.
Grave Liner (Outer Container, Vault)	A concrete cover that fits over a casket in a grave to minimize ground settling. Some liners cover the tops and sides of the casket. Vaults completely enclose the casket.
Health Care Power of Attorney	An advance directive naming another person as your agent or proxy to make medical decisions for you, if you should become unable to make them for yourself. It becomes active any time you are unconscious or are unable to make medical decisions. Also known as Durable Power of Attorney for Health Care, Health Care Power of Attorney, and Health Care Proxy.
Health Care Proxy	An advance directive naming another person as your agent or proxy to make medical decisions for you, if you should become unable to make them for yourself. It becomes active any time you are unconscious or are unable to make medical decisions. Also known as Durable Power of Attorney for Health Care, Health Care Power of Attorney, and Health Care Surrogate Designation.

Health Care Surrogate Designation	An advance directive naming another person as your agent or proxy to make medical decisions for you, if you should become unable to make them for yourself. It becomes active any time you are unconscious or are unable to make medical decisions. Also known as Durable Power of Attorney for Health Care, Health Care Power of Attorney, and Health Care Proxy.
Holographic Will	A handwritten will. To be valid, a holographic will must be written, dated, and signed in the handwriting of the person making the will. Holographic wills are legal in about 25 states.
Hospice	Provides comfort and support to terminally ill patients and their families, its goal being to improve the quality of the remainder of the patient's life. Also offers bereavement and counseling services to families before and after a patient's death.
Internment	Inurnment, entombment, or burial in the ground.
Inurnment	The placement of cremains in an urn.
Intestate Succession	The process by which state law determines what happens to your property if you fail to choose an executor to ensure your prop-

erty is distributed according to your wishes.

Keepsake Jewelry

Jewelry used to hold a small portion of cremains, when only a portion of ashes will be scattered, or when family members opt to divide the cremains among themselves.

Keepsake Urn

An urn used to hold a small portion of cremains, when only a portion of ashes will be scattered, or when family members opt to divide the cremains among themselves.

Letter of Intent

A list of items with corresponding beneficiaries with which you can adjoin to your will to specify who gets what.

Living Will

An advance directive that specifies the kind of medical care you want or do not want if you are unable to make your own decisions. It only takes effect when you are terminally ill.

Memorial Service

A service during which the body is not in attendance. Memorial services are usually held for those whom are buried elsewhere or have been cremated.

Niche

A recessed compartment designed to hold an urn in a columbarium. Niches vary in size, and may have glass, marble, bronze, or granite fronts.

Payable-on-Death Certificate (POD) A type of savings account usually held in joint names: the funeral home's and yours. When you die, the account automatically belongs to the funeral home.

Prearranging Comprises preplanning and prefunding.

Prefunding Different methods of investing and paying for your funeral plans.

Preneed Funeral Contract A contract containing a complete description and current price of the goods and services you are purchasing, as well as what goods and services are required, the rights and obligations of all parties to the contract, the relationship between the entity providing the funding and the funeral home providing the goods and services, etc.

Preplanning Planning ahead for your death. Preplanning includes decisions about whether to be buried or cremated and type of casket or urn, e.g., but does not consider how your plans will be paid for.

Probate A legal process that takes place after someone dies, during which an executor must prove the validity of the will and present the court with a list of property, debts, and beneficiaries so that the court will authorize the executor to sell off assets, pay debts and taxes, and divide the remaining assets among the beneficiaries named in the will. Commonly takes a year. "The means of 'avoiding' probate exist, including creating trusts in which all possessions are handled by a trustee, making lifetime gifts or putting all substantial property in joint tenancy with an automatic right of survivorship in the joint owner. Even if there is a will, probate may not be necessary if the estate is small with no real estate title to be transferred or all of the estate is either jointly owned or community property. Reasons for avoiding probate are the fees set by statute and/or the court (depending on state laws) for attorneys, executors and administrators, the need to publish notices, court hearings, paperwork, the public nature of the proceedings and delays while waiting for creditors to file claims even when the deceased owed no one."[80]

Professional Fee

The funeral home's cost of doing business. Defined by the Federal Trade Commission (FTC) as allowable coverage for the basic services of the funeral director and staff, furnished by the funeral provider in arranging any funeral, such as conducting the arrangements conference, planning the funeral, obtaining necessary permits, and placing obituary notices. It is the only funeral provider fee permitted for services, facilities, or unallocated overhead. It is nondeclinable, unless otherwise permitted by law. Also known as the Basic Services Fee.

Scattering Garden

An area in a cemetery where loved ones may scatter ashes. The names of those whose remains have been scattered in the garden are inscribed on a memorial plaque, wall, or work of art.

Statement of Goods and Services

An itemized statement that clearly identifies what goods and services are required, explains why they are required, provides cost information, and includes required disclosures regarding legal requirements, embalming, and cash advance items. The Federal Trade Commission (FTC) requires funeral homes to provide you with one.

Summary Notice

More commonly known as an Explanation of Benefits (EOB), a statement mailed to a patient after a claim has been submitted to Medicare. It contains such information as the claim number, service provided, physician's name, amount charged, etc.

Traditional Funeral

A typically expensive funeral that usually includes a viewing or visitation, a formal funeral service, and a hearse to transport the body to the funeral site and cemetery.

Totten Trust

A bank account in your name for which you name a beneficiary. Upon your death, the money transfers automatically to the beneficiary.

Trust

"An entity created to hold assets for the benefit of certain persons or entities, with a trustee managing the trust (and often holding title on behalf of the trust). Most trusts are founded by the persons (called trustors, settlors and/or donors) who execute a written declaration of trust which establishes the trust and spells out the terms and conditions upon which it will be conducted. The declaration also names the original trustee or trustees, successor trustees or means to choose future trustees. The assets of the trust are usually given to the trust by the creators, although assets may be added by others. During the life of the trust, profits and, sometimes, a portion of the principal (called 'corpus') may be distributed to the beneficiaries, and at some time in the future (such as the death of the last trustor or settlor) the remaining assets will be distributed to beneficiaries. A trust may take the place of a will and avoid probate (management of an estate with court supervision) by providing for distribution of all assets originally owned by the trustors or settlors upon their death."[81]

Urn

A container for cremains.

Urn Garden

An area in a cemetery or memorial park designated for internment of cremains.

Will

"A written document which leaves the estate of the person who signed the will to named persons or entities (beneficiaries, legatees, divisees) including portions or percentages of the estate, specific gifts, creation of trusts for management and future distribution of all or a portion of the estate (a testamentary trust). A will usually names an executor (and possibly substitute executors) to manage the estate, states the authority and obligations of the executor in the management and distribution of the estate, sometimes gives funeral and/or burial instructions, nominates guardians of minor children and spells out other terms. To be valid the will must be signed by the person who made it (testator), be dated (but an incorrect date will not invalidate the will) and witnessed by two people (except in Vermont which requires three). In some states the witnesses must be disinterested, or in some states, a gift to a witness is void, but the will is valid. A will totally in the handwriting of the testator, signed and dated (a "holographic will") but without witnesses, is valid in many, but not all, states. If the will (also called a Last Will and Testament) is still in force at the time of the death of the testator (will writer), and there is a substantial estate and/or real estate, then the will must be probated (approved by the court, managed and distributed by the executor under court supervision). If there is no executor named or the executor is dead or unable or unwilling to serve, an administrator ("with will annexed") will be appointed by the court. A written amendment or addition to a will is called a "codicil" and must be signed, dated and witnessed just as is a will, and must refer to the original will it amends. If there is no estate, including the situation in which the assets have all been placed in a trust, then the will need not be probated."[82]

APPENDIX B:
USEFUL WEBSITES

AARP offers a wide variety of resources and information on bereavement issues for adults of all ages and their families. Services include: one-to-one peer outreach, a grief course, bereavement support groups, informational booklets and brochures, and online support.

http://www.aarp.org/griefandloss/

ABANetwork™, an American Bar Association website, is an excellent source of legal information.

http://www.abanet.org/

Advanced Funeral Planning, LLC, website is a premier source of information pertaining to planning a funeral in advance, and is cited numerous times herein.

http://www.advancedfuneralplanning.com/

Americans for Better Care of the Dying (ABCD) is dedicated to improving end-of-life care.

http://www.abcd-caring.org/

Bereavement Hospitality Services, Inc., provides preplanned bereavement-related travel services at bereavement, compassion fares, or sympathy fares.

http://www.bereavetravel.com/

Beyond Indigo is a web site devoted to "changing the way you feel about grief and loss."

http://www.beyondindigo.com/

BuyCaskets.com offers a selection of caskets manufactured by the three largest manufacturers of caskets and related funeral products.

http://www.buycaskets.com/

BuyUrns.com offers a selection of urns, including companion urns, scattering urns, and keepsake urns.

http://www.buyurns.com/

Casketxpress.com offers 20 categories of caskets online.

http://casketxpress.com/

Council of Better Business Bureaus, Inc.

http://www.bbb.org/

Cremation Association of North America website offers consumer brochures and information.

http://www.cremationassociation.org/

Department of Veterans Affairs National Cemetery Administration website provides information on the VA's national cemeteries and other benefits.

http://www.cem.va.gov/

Federal Trade Commission, which regulates the funeral industry. Offers *Funerals: A Consumer Guide* in .pdf format.

http://www.ftc.gov/bcp/conline/pubs/services/funeral.pdf

Funeral Consumers Alliance, a nonprofit educational organization, supports increased funeral consumer protection. Affiliated with Funeral and Memorial Society of America (FAMSA).

http://www.funerals.org/

Funeral Etiquette page provided by Turner & Porter Funeral Directors Limited.

http://www.turnerporter.ca/etiquet.htm

Funeral Service Foundation, The, through charitable gifts and grants, provides excellent resources for public awareness and education. Cited numerous times herein.

http://www.funeralservicefoundation.org/

GriefNet.org is an Internet community of persons dealing with grief, death, and major loss with 37 e-mail support groups and two web sites.

http://www.rivendell.org/

Hospice Foundation of America assists professionals and the families they serve in issues relating to caregiving, terminal illness, loss, and bereavement.

http://www.hospicefoundation.org/

International Cemetery and Funeral Association, a nonprofit association of cemeteries, funeral homes, crematories, and monument retailers that provides informal mediation of consumer complaints.

http://www.icfa.org/

International Order of the Golden Rule is an international association of independent funeral homes.

http://www.ogr.org/

Jewish Funeral Directors of America is an international association of funeral homes serving the Jewish community.

http://www.jfda.org/

KIDSAID is a safe place for kids to share, and to help each other deal with grief about any of their losses. It is owned and operated by GriefNet.

http://kidsaid.com/

Law.com Dictionary, "The Real Life Dictionary of the Law" by Gerald and Kathleen Hill. Published by General Publishing Group. One of Paul's favorites.

http://dictionary.law.com/

LegalZoom.com helps you create legal documents online.

http://www.legalzoom.com/

National Funeral Directors and Morticians Association is a national association comprised primarily of African-American funeral providers.

http://www.nfdma.com/

National Funeral Directors Asociation (NFDA) website offers excellent consumer resources in areas of preneed, preplanning, pre-paying, coping with grief, etc.

http://www.nfda.org/resources/

National Hospice Foundation (NHPCO) is a charitable organization dedicated to broadening understanding of hospice.

http://www.hospiceinfo.org/

National Selected Morticians is a national association of funeral firms that have agreed to comply with its Code of Good Funeral Practice.

http://www.nsm.org/

Neptune Society is a company that offers cremation services. Scattering of ashes at sea is common for many "members." — http://www.neptunesociety.com/

Nolo.com, an excellent source of legal information. — http://www.nolo.com/

Richard Lamb Funeral Service & Resource Center provides funeral services and merchandise. Website offers superb consumer education and funeral planning pages. — http://www.richardlamb.com/

SeniorCareWeb.com, a website for seniors and caregivers providing information on health, family, legal, and financial issues. — http://www2.seniorcareweb.com/

Social Security Administration's Social Security Online, the official website of the SSA., provides important benefits information and a local office locator. — http://www.ssa.gov/

State of Florida Agency for Health Care Administration website provides useful information for residents of Florida. — http://www.fdhc.state.fl.us/

Urnxpress.com offers hundreds of styles of urns at wholesale prices. — http://www.urnxpress.com/

U. S. Department of Health and Human Services Health Resources and Services Administration (HRSA) organ donation website.	http://www.organdonor.gov/
Virtual Hospital, a digital library created at the University of Iowa to make the Internet a useful medical reference and health promotion tool for health care providers and patients.	http://www.vh.org/
What You Need to Know About™ Death and Dying, from About.com, provides extensive information on the subject, including teen grief, child loss, eulogies, funerals, wills, religion, inspiration, etc.	http://www.dying.about.com/

APPENDIX C: STATE LICENSING BOARDS

ALABAMA Board of Funeral Service
770 Washington Avenue, Suite 226
Montgomery, AL 36130
(334) 242-4049

ALASKA Division of Occupational Licensing
Mortuary Science Section
P. O. Box 110806
Juneau, AK 99811-0806
(907) 465-2695

ARIZONA State Board of Funeral Directors and Embalmers
1400 W. Washington, Room 230
Phoenix, AZ 85007
(602) 542-3095

ARKANSAS State Board of Embalmers and Funeral Directors
101 E. Capitol, Suite 113
Little Rock, AR 72201
(501) 682-0574

CALIFORNIA Cemetery and Funeral Program
400 R Street, Suite 3040
Sacramento, CA 95814
(916) 322-7737

COLORADO Funeral Service Board
7853 E. Arapahoe Court, #2100
Englewood, CO 80112
(303)-694-4728
www.cofda.org

CONNECTICUT Embalmer/Funeral Director Licensure
Department of Public Health
410 Capitol Avenue, MS #12APP
P. O. Box 340308
Hartford, CT 06134
(860) 509-7569

DELAWARE Board of Funeral Service
Cannon Building, Suite 203
861 Silver Lake Boulevard
Dover, DE 19904
(302) 739-4522

DISTRICT OF COLOMBIA Board of Funeral Directors
Occupational and Professional Licensing Administration
614 H Street N. W., Room 923
Washington, DC 20001
(202) 727-7473

FLORIDA Board of Funeral Directors and Embalmers
1940 N. Monroe Street, Suite 60
Tallahassee, FL 32399-0745
(850) 488-8690

GEORGIA State Examining Boards
237 Coliseum Drive
Macon, GA 31217
(478) 207-1460

HAWAII Sanitation Branch
Department of Health
591 Ala Moana
Honolulu, HI 96813
(808) 586-8000

IDAHO State Board of Morticians
Bureau of Occupational Licenses
Owyhee Plaza
1109 Main Street, Suite 220
Boise, ID 83702
(208) 334-3233
(208) 334-3945
www.state.id.us/ibol/mor.htm

ILLINOIS Professional Services Section
Department of Professional Regulation
320 W. Washington Street
Springfield, IL 62786
(217) 785-0800

INDIANA Funeral Service Board
302 W. Washington Avenue, Room E-034
Indianapolis, IN 46204
(317) 232-7215

IOWA Board of Mortuary Science
Iowa Department of Public Health
321 E. 12th Street
Des Moines, IA 50319-0075
(515) 281-4287

KANSAS State Board of Mortuary Arts
700 S. W. Jackson, Suite 904
Topeka, KS 66603-3733
(785) 296-3980

KENTUCKY State Board of Embalmers and Funeral Directors
P. O. Box 324
Crestwood, KY 40014
(502) 241-3918

LOUISIANA State Board of Embalmers and Funeral Directors
P. O. Box 8757
Metairie, LA 70011
(504) 838-5109

MAINE Board of Funeral Service
State House Station 35
Augusta, ME 04333
(207) 582-8723

MARYLAND State Board of Morticians
Department of Health and Mental Hygiene
4201 Patterson Avenue
Baltimore, MD 21215-2299
(410) 764-4792

MASSACHUSETTS Board of Funeral Service
Leverett Saltonstall Building
100 Cambridge Street
Boston, MA 02202
(617) 727-1718
www.state.ma.us/reg/boards

MICHIGAN Department of Consumer
Board of Examiners in Mortuary Science
P. O. Box 30018
Lansing, MI 48909
(517) 241-9258

MINNESOTA Mortuary Science Section
121 E. 7th Place
P. O. Box 64975
St. Paul, MN 55164-0975
(651) 282-3829

MISSISSIPPI State Board of Funeral Service
1307 E. Fortification
Jackson, MS 39202
(601) 354-6903
www.msfuneralboard.com

MISSOURI State Board of Embalmers and Funeral Directors
P. O. Box 423
Jefferson City, MO 65102-0423
(573) 751-0813

MONTANA Board of Funeral Service
P. O. Box 200513
Helena, MT 59620-0513
(406) 444-5433

NEBRASKA Department of Health and Human Services Credentialing Division
P. O. Box 94986
301 Centennial Mall South
Lincoln, NE 68509
(402) 471-2117

NEVADA Board of Funeral Directors and Embalmers
305 N. Carson Street, #201
Carson City, NV 89701
(775) 882-3005

NEW HAMPSHIRE Board of Registration of Funeral Directors and Embalmers
Health and Welfare Building
6 Hazen Drive
Concord, NH 03301-6527
(603) 271-4648

NEW JERSEY State Board of Mortuary Science
P. O. Box 45009, Room 513
Newark, NJ 07101
(973) 504-6425

NEW MEXICO State Board of Thanatopractice
P. O. Box 25101
Santa Fe, NM 87504
(505) 476-7090

NEW YORK Bureau of Funeral Directing
New York State Department of Health
Hedley Park Place
433 River Street, Suite 303
Troy, NY 12180
(518) 402-0785

NORTH CAROLINA Board of Mortuary Science
P. O. Box 27368
Raleigh, NC 27611-7368
(919) 733-9380

NORTH DAKOTA Board of Embalmers
P. O. Box 633
Devils Lake, ND 58301
(701) 662-2511

OHIO Board of Embalmers and Funeral Directors
77 S. High Street, 16th Floor
Columbus, OH 43226-0313
(614) 466-4252
www.state.oh.us

OKLAHOMA State Board of Embalmers and Funeral Directors
4545 N. Lincoln Boulevard, Suite 175
Oklahoma City, OK 73105
(405) 525-0158

OREGON State Mortuary and Cemetery Board
Portland State Office Building, Suite 430
800 N. E. Oregon Street, Box #19
Portland, OR 97232
(503) 731-4040

PENNSYLVANIA State Board of Funeral Directors
P. O. Box 2649
Harrisburg, PA 17105-2649
(717) 783-3397

RHODE ISLAND Division of Professional Regulation
State Health Department Building, Room 104
3 Capitol Hill
Providence, RI 02908
(401) 222-2827

SOUTH CAROLINA State Board of Funeral Service
Department of Labor, Licensing and Regulation
P. O. Box 11329
Columbia, SC 29211-1329
(803) 896-4494
(803) 896-4497

SOUTH DAKOTA Board of Funeral Service
132 E. Illinois
Spearfish, SD 57783
(605) 741-2378

TENNESSEE State Board of Funeral Directors and Embalmers
500 James Robertson Parkway
Nashville, TN 37243-1144
(615) 741-2378

TEXAS Funeral Service Commission
510 S. Congress, Suite 206
Austin, TX 78704-7222
(512) 936-2474

UTAH Department of Professional Licensing
P. O. Box 146741
Salt Lake City, UT 84114-6741
(801) 530-6396
www.commerce.state.ut.us

VERMONT Board of Funeral Service
Office of Professional Regulation
Pavilion Building
109 State Street
Montpelier, VT 05609-1106
(802) 828-3256

VIRGINIA Department of Health Professions
Board of Funeral Directors
6606 W. Broad Street, 4th Floor
Richmond, VA 23230
(840) 662-9907

WASHINGTON Funeral and Cemetery Office
Business and Professions Divisions
P. O. Box 9012

Olympia, WA 98507-9012
(360) 586-4905

WEST VIRGINIA Board of Embalmers and Funeral Directors
179 Summers Street, Suite 305
Charleston, WV 25301
(304) 558-0302

WISCONSIN Department of Regulation and Licensing
Funeral Directors Examining Board
P. O. Box 8935
Madison, WI 53708
(608) 266-5511

WYOMING State Board of Embalming
2020 Carey Avenue, Suite 201
Cheyenne, WY 82002
(307) 777-7788

ENDNOTES

1. Federal Trade Commission (FTC). (2002). *Funerals: A Consumer Guide.* Retrieved September 6, 2002 from http://www.ftc.gov/bcp/conline/pubs/services/funeral.pdf

2. American Academy of Family Physicians (1994). Advance directives and do-not-resuscitate orders: What you need to know. Retrieved August 21, 2001 from http://www.vh.org/Patients/IHB/FamilyPractice/AFP/November/NovTwo.html

3. State of Florida Agency for Health Care Administration (1999). Health care advance directives: Your right to decide and make your wishes known. Retrieved from http://www.fdhc.state.fl.us

4. State of Florida Agency for Health Care Administration (1999). Health care Advance directives: Your right to decide and make your wishes known. Retrieved from http://www.fdhc.state.fl.us

5. American Academy of Family Physicians (1994). Advance directives and do-not-resuscitate orders: What you need to know. Retrieved August 21, 2001 from http://www.vh.org/Patients/IHB/FamilyPractice/AFP/November/NovTwo.html

6. Sabatino, Charles P. 10 legal myths about advance medical directives. Washington, DC: Commission on Legal Problems of the Elderly, American Bar Association. Retrieved from http://www.abanet.org

7. Sabatino, Charles P. 10 legal myths about advance medical directives. Washington, DC: Commission on Legal Problems of the Elderly, American Bar Association. Retrieved from http://www.abanet.org

8. Sabatino, Charles P. 10 legal myths about advance medical directives. Washington, DC: Commission on Legal Problems of the Elderly, American Bar Association. Retrieved from http://www.abanet.org

9. American Academy of Family Physicians (1994). Advance directives and do-not-resuscitate orders: What you need to know. Retrieved August 21, 2001 from http://www.vh.org/Patients/IHB/FamilyPractice/AFP/November/ NovTwo.html

10. Sabatino, Charles P. 10 legal myths about advance medical directives. Washington, DC: Commission on Legal Problems of the Elderly, American Bar Association. Retrieved from http://www.abanet.org

11. State of Florida Agency for Health Care Administration. (1999). Health care advance directives: Your right to decide and make your wishes known. Retrieved from http://www.fdhc.state.fl.us

12. State of Florida Agency for Health Care Administration. (1999). Health care advance directives: Your right to decide and make your wishes known. Retrieved from http://www.fdhc.state.fl.us

13. DCMSonline. (2001). Designation of health care surrogate. Retrieved August 21, 2001 from http://www.dcmsonline.org/designat.htm

14. The basis for this section comes from an article by Peter Weaver entitled "10 Good Reasons Why You Should Have a Will" on Thirdage.com, a website sponsored by Merrill Lynch. Retrieved May 23, 2001 from http://aol.thirdage.com/features/money/good-will/index.html

15. Nolo. (2001). Wills FAQ. Retrieved August 9, 2001 from http://www.nolo.com/encyclopedia/articles/ep/epwill_faq.html

16. Weaver, Peter. 10 good reasons why you should have a will. Retrieved May 23, 2001 from http://aol.thirdage.com/features/money/goodwill/index.html

17. Nolo. (2001). Wills FAQ. Retrieved August 9, 2001 from http://www.nolo.com/encyclopedia/articles/ep/epwill_faq.html

18. Nolo. (2001). Wills FAQ. Retrieved August 9, 2001 from http://www.nolo.com/encyclopedia/articles/ep/epwill_faq.html

19. Federal Trade Commission (FTC). (2002). *Funerals: A Consumer Guide.* Retrieved September 6, 2002 from http://www.ftc.gov/bcp/conline/pubs/services/funeral.pdf

20. Lamb, R. (2001). What are the benefits of pre-need planning? Retrieved June 8, 2001 from http://www.richardlamb.com/Preneed/BENEFITS.ASP

21. Consumer Reports (2001). Final arrangements. *Consumer Reports Online*, May 2001. Retrieved June 8, 2001 from http://www.con-sumerreports.org

22. Funeral Service Educational Foundation (2000). Buyer's guide to preneed funeral planning. Retrieved June 8, 2001 from http://www.fsef.org/consumerassistance/buyerguide.php

23. Funeral Service Educational Foundation (2000). Buyer's guide to preneed funeral planning. Retrieved June 8, 2001 from http://www.fsef.org/consumerassistance/buyerguide.php

24. USA Today (2001). Snapshot. Retrieved August 21, 2001 from http://www.usatoday.com/snapshot/news/nsnap115.htm

25. Cremation Association of North America (1999). Cremation data by state and predictions to 2000 and 2010.

26. See "Cremation vs. Burial: Christian Controversy" at http://www.religioustolerance.org/crematio.htm

27. Cremation Association of North America. (2001). Cremation memorial options. Retrieved August 21, 2001 from http://www.beyondindigo.com/articles/article.php/artID/315

28. Cremation Association of North America. (2001). Cremation memorial options. Retrieved August 21, 2001 from http://www.beyondindigo.com/articles/article.php/artID/315

29. Cremation Association of North America. (2001). Cremation memorial options. Retrieved August 21, 2001 from http://www.beyondindigo.com/articles/article.php/artID/315

30. Cremation Association of North America. (2001). Cremation memorial options. Retrieved August 21, 2001 from http://www.beyondindigo.com/articles/article.php/artID/315

31. See "Senate Hearing Slams Funeral Service" by Beacham McDonald at http://www.ogr.org/news_views.cgi?id=3

32. Federal Trade Commission (FTC). (2002). *Funerals: A Consumer Guide.* Retrieved September 6, 2002 from http://www.ftc.gov/bcp/conline/pubs/services/funeral.pdf

33. Federal Trade Commission (FTC). (2002). *Funerals: A Consumer Guide.* Retrieved September 6, 2002 from http://www.ftc.gov/bcp/conline/pubs/services/funeral.pdf

34. Funeral Service Educational Foundation (2000). Buyer's guide to preneed funeral planning. Retrieved June 8, 2001 from http://www.fsef.org/consumerassistance/buyerguide.php

35. Funeral Service Educational Foundation (2000). Buyer's guide to preneed funeral planning. Retrieved June 8, 2001 from http://www.fsef.org/consumerassistance/buyerguide.php

36. Funeral Service Educational Foundation (2000). Buyer's guide to preneed funeral planning. Retrieved June 8, 2001 from http://www.fsef.org/consumerassistance/buyerguide.php

37. Funeral Service Educational Foundation (2000). Buyer's guide to preneed funeral planning. Retrieved June 8, 2001 from http://www.fsef.org/consumerassistance/buyerguide.php

38. Funeral Service Educational Foundation (2000). Buyer's guide to preneed funeral planning. Retrieved June 8, 2001 from http://www.fsef.org/consumerassistance/buyerguide.php

39. Funeral Service Educational Foundation (2000). Buyer's guide to preneed funeral planning. Retrieved June 8, 2001 from http://www.fsef.org/consumerassistance/buyerguide.php

40. Consumer Reports (2001). Final arrangements. *Consumer Reports Online,* May 2001. Retrieved June 8, 2001 from http://www.consumerreports.org

41. Federal Trade Commission (FTC). (2002). *Funerals: A Consumer Guide.* Retrieved September 6, 2002 from http://www.ftc.gov/bcp/conline/pubs/services/funeral.pdf

42. Federal Trade Commission (FTC). (2002). *Funerals: A Consumer Guide.* Retrieved September 6, 2002 from http://www.ftc.gov/bcp/conline/pubs/services/funeral.pdf

43. Funeral Service Educational Foundation (2000). Buyer's guide to preneed funeral planning. Retrieved June 8, 2001 from http://www.fsef.org/consumerassistance/buyerguide.php

44. Advance Funeral Planning. (2001). Survivor benefits. Retrieved June 8, 2001 from http://www.advancedfuneralplanning.com/social.htm

45. SeniorCareWeb.com (2001). The Totten Trust. Retrieved August 9, 2001 from http://www2.seniorcareweb.com/senior/financial/assets_and_tru/fintotten.htm

46. Advance Funeral Planning. (2001). Survivor benefits. Retrieved June 8, 2001 from http://www.advancedfuneralplanning.com/trusts.htm

47. Funeral Service Educational Foundation (2000). Buyer's guide to preneed funeral planning. Retrieved June 8, 2001 from http://www.fsef.org/consumerassistance/buyerguide.php

48. Funeral Service Educational Foundation (2000). Buyer's guide to preneed funeral planning. Retrieved June 8, 2001 from http://www.fsef.org/consumerassistance/buyerguide.php

49. Weathersby, T. (2001). Death and dying. Retrieved August 9, 2001 from http://dying.about.com/library/weekly/aa072897.htm

50. Weathersby, T. (2001). Death and dying: Denial and isolation phase of grief. Retrieved August 9, 2001 from http://dying.about.com/library/weekly/aa072897.htm

51. Weathersby, T. (2001). Death and dying: Anger phase of grief. Retrieved August 9, 2001 from http://dying.about.com/library/weekly/aa080497.htm

52. Weathersby, T. (2001). Death and dying: Bargaining phase of grief. Retrieved August 9, 2001 from http://dying.about.com/library/weekly/aa081197.htm

53. Weathersby, T. (2001). Death and dying: Depression phase of grief. Retrieved August 9, 2001 from http://dying.about.com/library/weekly/aa081997.htm

54. Weathersby, T. (2001). Death and dying: Acceptance phase of grief. Retrieved August 9, 2001 from http://dying.about.com/library/weekly/aa082697.htm

55. Parachin, V. (2001). Grief relief: Loss impacts people in different ways. Retrieved June 8, 2001 from http://www.nfda.org/resources/grief/2001/feb.html

56. Craig, G. J. (1999). *Human Development.* Upper Saddle River, NJ: Prentice Hall.

57. Hospice Foundation of America. (2001). What is hospice? Retrieved August 22, 2001 from http://www.hospicefoundation.org/what_is/

58. Nolo. (2001). Probate FAQ. Retreived August 9, 2001 from http://www.nolo.com/encyclopedia/articles/ep/ep28-31.html

59. Nolo. (2001). Probate FAQ. Retreived August 9, 2001 from http://www.nolo.com/encyclopedia/articles/ep/ep28-31.html

60. Nolo. (2001). Probate FAQ. Retreived August 9, 2001 from http://www.nolo.com/encyclopedia/articles/ep/ep28-31.html

61. Nolo. (2001). Probate FAQ. Retreived August 9, 2001 from http://www.nolo.com/encyclopedia/articles/ep/ep28-31.html

62. Nolo. (2001). Probate FAQ. Retreived August 9, 2001 from http://www.nolo.com/encyclopedia/articles/ep/ep28-31.html

63. Advance Funeral Planning. (2001). Survivor benefits. Retrieved June 8, 2001 from http://www.advancedfuneralplanning.com/social.htm

64. Advance Funeral Planning. (2001). Survivor benefits. Retrieved June 8, 2001 from http://www.advancedfuneralplanning.com/social.htm

65. Advance Funeral Planning. (2001). Survivor benefits. Retrieved June 8, 2001 from http://www.advancedfuneralplanning.com/social.htm

66. Advance Funeral Planning. (2001). Survivor benefits. Retrieved June 8, 2001 from http://www.advancedfuneralplanning.com/social.htm

67. Advance Funeral Planning. (2001). Survivor benefits. Retrieved June 8, 2001 from http://www.advancedfuneralplanning.com/social.htm

68. Federal Trade Commission (FTC). (2002). *Funerals: A Consumer Guide*. Retrieved September 6, 2002 from http://www.ftc.gov/bcp/conline/pubs/services/funeral.pdf

69. Federal Trade Commission (FTC). (2002). *Funerals: A Consumer Guide*. Retrieved September 6, 2002 from http://www.ftc.gov/bcp/conline/pubs/services/funeral.pdf

70. Federal Trade Commission (FTC). (2002). *Funerals: A Consumer Guide*. Retrieved September 6, 2002 from http://www.ftc.gov/bcp/conline/pubs/services/funeral.pdf

71. Advance Funeral Planning. (2001). Survivor benefits. Retrieved June 8, 2001 from http://www.advancedfuneralplanning.com/veterans.htm

72. Advance Funeral Planning. (2001). Survivor benefits. Retrieved June 8, 2001 from http://www.advancedfuneralplanning.com/veterans.htm

73. Advance Funeral Planning. (2001). Survivor benefits. Retrieved June 8, 2001 from http://www.advancedfuneralplanning.com/social.htm

74. Advance Funeral Planning. (2001). Survivor benefits. Retrieved June 8, 2001 from http://www.advancedfuneralplanning.com/social.htm

75. Federal Trade Commission (FTC). (2002). *Funerals: A Consumer Guide.* Retrieved September 6, 2002 from http://www.ftc.gov/bcp/conline/pubs/services/funeral.pdf

76. Federal Trade Commission (FTC). (2002). *Funerals: A Consumer Guide.* Retrieved September 6, 2002 from http://www.ftc.gov/bcp/conline/pubs/services/funeral.pdf

77. Federal Trade Commission (FTC). (2002). *Funerals: A Consumer Guide.* Retrieved September 6, 2002 from http://www.ftc.gov/bcp/conline/pubs/services/funeral.pdf

78. Federal Trade Commission (FTC). (2002). *Funerals: A Consumer Guide.* Retrieved September 6, 2002 from http://www.ftc.gov/bcp/conline/pubs/services/funeral.pdf

79. Hill, G., & Hill. K. (2000). *Law.com Dictionary.* Santa Montica, CA: General Publishing Group. Retrieved September 5, 2002 from http://dictionary.law.com/

80. Hill, G., & Hill. K. (2000). *Law.com Dictionary*. Santa Montica, CA: General Publishing Group. Retrieved September 5, 2002 from http://dictionary.law.com/

81. Hill, G., & Hill. K. (2000). *Law.com Dictionary*. Santa Montica, CA: General Publishing Group. Retrieved September 5, 2002 from http://dictionary.law.com/

82. Hill, G., & Hill. K. (2000). *Law.com Dictionary*. Santa Montica, CA: General Publishing Group. Retrieved September 5, 2002 from http://dictionary.law.com/

0-595-24981-7